Praise for *Raising Lea*

I wish that I had read *Raising Leaders* 20 or more years ago, when I first started out managing people. Wendy outlines simple and relatable strategies for the successful management and development of teams. Wendy's generous and courageous sharing of her own personal life experiences clearly demonstrate the alignment of raising children and leaders.

Greg Nielsen – General Manager, Retread Business, Bandag Manufacturing Pty Ltd

Wendy is someone who walks her talk and leads from the heart. Having led in this authentic way for many years, she is positioned to train leaders with clarity and results. In *Raising Leaders*, she brings to life the parallels of parenting and leadership in a relatable and relevant way. Practical application of her wisdom from parenting lessons and as an executive leader/executive coach makes this book a valuable guide for all leaders.

Nicky Angelone – Flourish Mindfully

Wendy brings a style of coaching that is relevant and applicable for both personal and professional development and growth. She is able to break things down into simple relatable concepts, allowing her to connect in a manner that builds an inclusive, shared and valuable learning experience.

Mick O'Malley – Training Manager WPST

Wendy draws on examples from work, life and parenting to create an easy-to-follow guide for raising leaders. An outstanding resource for both new and experienced leaders.

Rob Elliot – Financial Services

Filled with insight, stories and humour, *Raising Leaders* expertly parallels parenting with developing cohesive teams, and shows how love, connection and safety are critical for success. A must-read for anyone looking to elevate their own leadership journey.

Gaye Wealthy – General Manager, People & Culture, Telecommunications Industry Ombudsman

After reading Wendy Born's first book *The Languages of Leadership* I couldn't wait to read her second book *Raising Leaders*. Wendy writes with such succinct clarity; the leadership learnings are immediate and can be implemented in your working life with a new-found confidence.

Steve Hayden – Business Development Manager, Workplace Simulation Training

It's easy for a leader to lose sight of the role they play within the environment they lead. Wendy's grounded advice for practical solutions draws on trust and confidence to nurture a leader and their mindset, encouraging reflection on decisions to encompass a holistic approach to better leadership.

Good leaders are created in an atmosphere of honesty, integrity and trust, those three traits are the benchmarks to develop a healthy culture.

Raising Leaders is an insightful read on the key steps for leaders to adopt in business at every level in an organisation and move future executives to a higher level of business agility and leadership.

Christopher Gray – CEO, The Haystack Group

From the very first event where I experienced Wendy's engaging speaking style, I realised that Wendy is about nurturing inspirational and courageous leadership. Wendy's unique break and rebuild programs have helped me and many business leaders and their teams reach their full potential.

Peter Sandor – CEO, Fearless

Raising LEADERS

Using the principles of parenting at work to become a great leader and create great leaders

WENDY BORN

First published in 2020 by Major Street Publishing Pty Ltd
PO Box 106, Highett, Vic. 3190
E: info@majorstreet.com.au
W: majorstreet.com.au
M: +61 421 707 983

A catalogue record for this
book is available from the
NATIONAL
LIBRARY   National Library of Australia
OF AUSTRALIA

ISBN: 978-0-6487530-5-6

Internal design by Production Works
Cover design by Simone Geary
Printed in Australia by McPhersons Printing Group

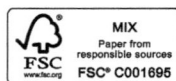

MIX
Paper from
responsible sources
FSC   FSC® C001695

10 9 8 7 6 5 4 3 2 1

CONTENTS

FOREWORD

When I talk to CEOs, senior executive teams or organisations about leadership and coaching, I make it very clear that parenting is a very similar role. In fact, parenting can be the most difficult role of all, as you – the parent – are connected emotionally to your child. Consequently, the child can press your emotional buttons in ways that a staff member or colleague or athlete cannot.

So, it was a great thrill to be asked by Wendy to write a foreword for this her second book on the broad topic of leadership. And I must say, the thrill did not diminish as I read her book.

I found myself grabbing and noting sentences, paragraphs, quotes, research articles like the infamous toilet-roll hoarding of COVID-19 – making sure I had everything on the 'shelves' that this book has to offer before anyone else could take its wisdom, its poignancy and its significant contribution to demystifying the secret codes of what good leadership IS.

Wendy takes you immediately into the realities of being a mother and parent, the daily juggling of everything at home;

then drop-off to school and the momentary release from these demands before entering the workspace and being confronted by similar demands from her adult staff.

As coach of the Australian Cricket team, and a father of five children, it would often amaze me that there were 35-year-old athletes in the dressing room who had travelled the globe, played in front of large crowds, met world acclaimed dignitaries and celebrities, yet sometimes their behaviour was adolescent, and my role moved from coaching to parenting.

Wendy refers to *déjà vecu* – you have 'lived the experience' already, as she says, '...*Like my children, my team plays one off against the other with the hope of getting in my good books and becoming my "favourite child". And, like my children, they sulk when they don't get their own way and complain about me behind my back...*'

Wendy sets further context for the book by introducing a Freud concept of *transference* along with the three ways of seeing using insight, plain sight and foresight. As she outlines, '*These are the overarching perspectives through which each chapter should be viewed so, as you read, please consider questions such as the following:*

- *What are the insights I can gain here? What insights do I need to develop?*

- *What is in plain sight that I can use, leverage, develop or take advantage of?*

- *What foresight do I need to develop, create or learn about?*'

So, having laid out some of the guidelines for reading the book, Wendy takes us through eight entertaining and easy-to-read chapters that provide insight, plain sight and foresight into how to be your best leader. You might not be awarded the 'best leader' title, but you are *your* best, and you deliver on that daily.

In Chapter 1, Wendy shares her brief experience as a young mother, with a less than cooperative child, joining a mothers group. Here she found she and son Harry just did not 'fit'. The group had their cliques, and none of the children seemed to be a problem. Her reflections as a leader, using her 'three ways of seeing' have shown her that society and organisations operate similarly. You are 'welcome' here, provided you do not question the system… because, by the way, this system has currency. It is politically correct. There is no room for someone who might have a different opinion, or wants to debate the existing norms.

Wendy concludes the chapter saying, '…*the conversation needs to continue, rather than forcing people further into their opposing corners. True inclusiveness is having the courage to accept people for what they are, how they behave and what they think, regardless of whether we agree or not. It's the ability to agree to disagree, but to keep talking, accepting others from all sides of faith, religion, sexuality, beliefs, values, thoughts and opinions, and forgiving even if it's hard to…*', and then she poses her reflective questioning.

The questions are included at the end of each chapter. If time does not permit you to answer these questions immediately, then I do encourage you to go back to the relevant chapters and invest in personal reflection.

Chapter 2 takes us further into understanding Wendy's perspectives on the similarities of parenting, families and leadership, as well as her model for creating an 'organisational family', which is strong, resilient, inclusive, innovative and successful. She uses the following five building blocks:

1. **Love:** This is the cornerstone of any family. It intimately binds people in relationships and is unconditional.

2. **Environment:** For an organisation or a team to grow, individuals must be given the opportunity to extend and stretch themselves. Just like children, the parent is always withdrawing, making themselves redundant, so that the child can learn, develop, mature and become more responsible and accountable. At the same time, good leadership and good parenting realise that errors will be made, the child will 'fall' – so they are there to catch, support, and get them back going again. As Wendy says, organisations refer to this as psychological safety.

3. **Health:** One of the support mechanisms for any child to grow is to be healthy – physically and mentally. This is no different to any person within a business or organisation – the research shows health and wellbeing are critical elements to productivity.

4. **Language:** In her first book, Wendy discusses the languages of leadership, which are the actions, behaviours and words used to influence, direct or control others. Leaders are always leading. Parents are always parenting. So being the example is a never-ending role to deliver.

5. **Vision:** Leaders inspire and challenge their teams with a picture of the future so that they work together to map the journey. Parents allow their children to dream about the future and help them put in place the building blocks that may allow the dreams to come true.

Finally, in this chapter, Wendy touches on one of the principal outcomes of her building blocks of leadership: 'being your own best coach'.

This is a term that I use to describe individuals who are very good, consistent decision-makers and, as a result, they achieve very good results. It is because they understand what is in their control, that they must do, to give themselves the best chance of being successful in the workplace or in life.

In chapters 3 to 7, Wendy expands on the principles with a wonderful blend of stories, research, personal experiences and questions. In chapter 5, there is a very personal account of Wendy's son, Harry, whose move to a changed educational system, which combined body and mind, had a real impact on his development and confidence. Taking the family example and showing how similar principles were applied at Johnson & Johnson, provides a very powerful 'seeing' of the benefits of health and wellbeing for individuals and organisations.

Language in chapter 6 is not to be rushed. Wendy is courageous in her incredible honesty, telling her life story in short movies and episodes. Understanding the six types of language used by her mother's husbands, has given her incredible insights to leadership from the positive and negative influences that significant others had in her life.

In chapter 7 we see again the connections that Wendy makes between parenting and family to leadership and teams. Recounting the story of a father and his two daughters alongside the founder of Patagonia, vividly demonstrates her final principle, '...*having purpose in the work you do and thinking strategically about how to achieve your goals, are the two elements in creating a great vision for your family and those you lead. The two are integral in determining the aspirational goals or the vision you want to achieve...*'.

The final chapter of the book is really the beginning for everyone's leadership reflection, exploration and continuing journey as she brings together her 'sightseeing' from chapter 1 across her five leadership principles, to provide a framework or roadmap for what she describes as 'all-the-time leadership'.

I am not the best of readers, although I enjoy reading something that makes sense due to its content; while, at the same time, making that content accessible and impactful through its storytelling.

I was unable to put this book down once I started. I know there is so much more contained in these pages, if you spend the time to reflect on the questions posed throughout the chapters.

Thank you, Wendy, for writing such a powerful addition to the leadership catalogue, and I do hope your readers gain as much from it as I did.

John Buchanan, former World Cup winning coach of the Australian national cricket team

ABOUT THE AUTHOR

Wendy Born helps leaders maximise their talents and strengths to achieve extraordinary results.

As an engaging facilitator, coach, speaker and author, she works with executives, senior leaders and leadership teams to create high-performance organisations that deliver that WOW-factor.

On any given day, leadership can be rewarding, frustrating, fun, risky and scary – all within the first hour. It can make you feel annoyed, furious, happy, proud and inspired, or like you want to curl up in a corner and rock back and forth.

With Wendy's guidance, leaders learn to build strong and enduring relationships to drive engagement and deliver on real strategic results that make the whole journey easier, more effective and even enjoyable.

Wendy is a highly experienced and recognised coach. She has more than 25 years' experience in corporate and management roles, including 10 years in senior leadership positions in finance, IT, retail, financial services, communications and government.

Wendy holds qualifications in human resources, finance and operations management, and is a certified personal and professional coach. She is also a graduate of the Harvard Kennedy School, Executive Education in 21st Century Leadership. Wendy's first book, *The Languages of Leadership: How to use your words, actions and behaviours to influence your team, peers and boss,* was published in 2019.

When she's not working, Wendy is continually challenged by her two kids, Harry and Lucy, who (without knowing it) teach her more about leadership than you ever would think possible.

She wouldn't have it any other way.

wendyborn.com.au

ACKNOWLEDGEMENTS

I enjoyed writing this book very much and found it easy to write. Perhaps because many of my personal stories and stories from loved ones are in here, it almost feels like a piece of me. However, I have also received much love, support and encouragement from those I love, including family, friends and colleagues, which has added to the pleasure of writing.

Firstly, thanks to my publisher, Lesley Williams, and the team at Major Street Publishing. I always feel so supported by you, and your ongoing encouragement means a great deal to me. Thanks also to Kelly Irving, whose editorial tools, templates and guidance are a constant source of reference for me. I could not have started my writing journey without you both. And thanks to Charlotte Duff, for pulling everything together and making it look like a real book. Your support and guidance has been invaluable.

Thanks to my partner, David Markham, whose constant source of stories, anecdotes, rhymes, songs and topics for new books keeps my mind stimulated and cheeks sore from laughter. Your love and unwavering faith in my abilities is a wonder and inspiration to me.

Thanks to my bestie, Alison Hawkins, for your calmness, common sense, rational advice and love. You're always there when I need you and you inspire me constantly. Also, thanks to my friend Michelle Sales – your support and encouragement with my business is something I will always be grateful for.

Thank you to the teachers and staff of the Frank Dando Sports Academy (FDSA) and Parkhill Primary School for allowing me the privilege of spending time with you and your students. In particular, thanks to Frank and Evelyn Dando, Ziad Zakharia, Paul Fyfield, Sam Battaglia, Jeff Newman and Mark Derrick from FDSA, and to Elaine Brady, Alex Davies, Andrea Crane and Desiree Schlack from Parkhill Primary School.

Thanks also to John Fauvel, Somone Johns, Dale Stevens, Marg Kitsakis, Warren and Annette Born, Narelle Slatyer, and David and Cas Blenkhorn for sharing your stories, experiences and insights into raising children and leading people. Some of your stories made the book while others didn't, but all provided valuable insight into its making.

Thanks to my children, Harry and Lucy, for your constant curiosity and laughter, and for helping me to understand how leadership extends way beyond just our work lives.

And finally, thanks to you, the reader of my book. I hope this helps you to be the leader you want to be and your leadership inspires those around you to be better people, making the world a better place.

INTRODUCTION: DÉJÀ VECU

'Muuuuuum, where are my shoes?'

'In the lounge room, beside the coffee table where you left them last night,' I reply.

'Mum, do I really have to go to school?'

'Yep.'

'Mum, what if I just have this one day off?'

'Nope.'

'Mum, can I just this once, pleeeeease?'

'No.'

As I retrieve shoes and associated socks, along with school bags, jumpers and hats, I reflect on the time, long ago, in a galaxy far, far away, when I actually had a name. I think it was Wendy. Great – back in this time, we are finally out the door.

'Mum, it's my turn for the front seat, remember?' Ah, yes, the prime real estate in a child's life is either a parent's lap or the front seat of the car. Over the next five minutes, I negotiate a peace deal between my two kids that results in me providing some kind of outlay in exchange for one child's possession of a three-minute ride up front.

The peace, however, is short-lived. 'Mum, when are we getting the gear I need for camp?' asks my son.

'Well, I will go through the list on the weekend and determine what you already have and then we will need to go shopping.'

'Mum, how come he gets to go shopping? I want to go shopping for stuff for me.'

Direct evidence suggests that the word 'mum' (in its numerous forms, styles and melodic practices) was the most used word in my household throughout 2019 (according to the survey of household residents at my address, 2019).

Finally, 45 minutes later, I arrive at the office and breathe a sigh of relief as I sit at my desk and turn my laptop on – at last, peace.

'Wendy, just before you start, can we talk about this problem I have with the guy who won't sign off on this deal? I'm not sure how to proceed.'

'Wendy, after you're done talking to Simon we need to talk about Michelle. She's really starting to get on my nerves about how I should be running this project.'

'Wendy, what should I do about… ?' 'Wendy, how come Andrew is… ?' 'Wendy, why is she… ?'

Why those you lead are like those you love

Ever had a similar situation – where you thought you were experiencing déjà vu by simply moving between two parts of your life? These kinds of feelings are very common, particularly when you lead people and raise children. To clarify, however, what you're actually feeling is *déjà vecu*, which is similar to déjà vu except that, whereas déjà vu is about having the illusion or feeling of having experienced something before, déjà vecu is the feeling of having 'already lived through' an experience (Funkhouser & Schredl, 2014). So when I arrived at work that day, déjà vecu kicked in because I'd lived through the exact same experience with my kids earlier.

The similarities between my team and my children are uncanny. Like my children, my team bring me their problems for me to sort out, either through fixing the problem myself or through providing them with the solution. Like my children, they complain about other members of the team or other people in different departments, as though I can provide some advice on how to deal with them, or admonish those people with some kind of punishment for behaving badly. Like my children, my team plays one off against the other with the hope of getting in my good books and becoming my 'favourite child'. And like my children, they sulk when they don't get their own way and complain about me behind my back.

When I have spoken to people about the concept of raising children being similar to leading people, I always receive a knowing nod. But you don't need to have raised children to understand this concept. We have all been raised by someone, and once you're an adult you eventually come to understand what you were like as a child and how you behaved towards your parents. I recall annoying my mother at times, asking for her to do things for me, whinging about not being allowed to do something, asking her to solve my problems for me and negotiating with her for something completely inane that, at the time, I couldn't possibly live without. Then we grow up, go to work and lead people.

Don't get me wrong – I'm not saying the people you work with and lead have the same maturity levels as children or act exactly like children. However, beneath our adult layers of maturity and social sophistication, the same needs, motivations and insecurities can emerge, and these influence how we act.

Many times, in the work I do with leaders, I hear them talk about how their team can be needy, dependent, play games (albeit political ones), behave like kids in the playground, whinge and sulk. Some leaders have described themselves or other leaders as acting like 'mother hens' towards their team members – always looking after their problems (personal or professional), solving things for them, looking after them, helping them and taking them under their wing. It's like their people are transferring their experiences and actions with their parents onto their leaders. Well, actually they are.

Sigmund Freud, Austrian neurologist and founder of psychoanalysis, developed the concept of transference in his book *Studies on Hysteria*, co-written with Josef Breuer and published in 1895. As noted in 'Transference' (www.goodtherapy.org), Freud described transference as a process in which 'deep, intense and often unconscious feelings' that someone has about one person are redirected towards another person – in Freud's case, these feelings were transferred onto Freud, within the therapeutic relationships he had with his patients. Transference is also common between people outside a therapeutic setting, and doesn't suggest someone has a mental health condition. The process is something that simply occurs, often unconsciously, between people and can help explain patterns of relationships that occur in our lives. An example of this may be when someone marries a person who displays similar behaviours to a parental figure or another significant influence in their life.

The common types of transference are:

- **Paternal:** When you look at someone as a father figure, and so may see them as authoritative, powerful and influential, and look to them for protection, guidance and patronage.

- **Maternal:** When you look at someone as a mother figure, and so may see them as caring, nurturing and loving, and look to them for comfort, support and encouragement.

- **Sibling:** When you look at someone as a brother or sister, and so may see them as supportive, encouraging and cooperative, and look to them for camaraderie, affiliation and connection.

- **Non-familial:** When you look at someone according to a particular version of what you expect of them instead of who they may actually be. This is typical when relying on stereotypes, such as expecting police officers to always uphold the law and clerics to always be saint-like.

Transference can be both positive and negative. For example, when an employee views their leader as similar to a positive parent or guardian, they will want to do things for them, and discretionary effort may increase in order to please them. A negative example could be where two employees are overly competitive – viewing each other as siblings competing for the attention of the parent figure, for example, and always wanting to outdo each other. Building your awareness of your own transferences will help you to manage this with those you lead.

Using your sight

By understanding how you look at others and what your expectations are of them, you will be able to make a connection between the significant influences in your life and those around you. These significant influences are the people who raised you, guided you and influenced you throughout your life. You may be able to identify behaviours, words, phrases and actions that you have in common with these people.

Through this awareness, you can then determine what countertransference (that is, your contribution to the transference) you would like others to have from you and adjust your behaviours to fit. For example, if you want your people to view you as a father figure, you could behave in an authoritative, strong and influential way. Author and businessman Stephen Covey once said, 'If you want to be trusted, be trustworthy' and the same applies here.

You need to think about how you would like others to see you, and then behave accordingly. To be respected, you need to be respectable; to be loved, you need to be lovable; and to be admired, you need to be admirable.

To act as you want to be seen, you need to have:

- **Insight** into both yourself and those you lead to create trust and connection as the foundation of your team. You also need insight into the importance of a positive attitude and mindset, and how good work–life balance works in with this, to see how these influence those around you.

- **Plain sight** to see what's in front of you and within your control as you practise good leadership, establish boundaries and expectations, and create a culture of accountability with your people. Through focusing on the things that you can control, you can feel empowered and in control of what you are doing.

- **Foresight** to determine your purpose, strategy and vision to guide a way into the future for you and your team. By creating a clear picture of the way forward, you set the direction, create purpose and meaning in the work you and your people do, and increase the probability of delivery.

As you progress further through this book, I encourage you to keep these three ways of seeing in mind. These are the overarching perspectives through which each chapter should be viewed, so, as you read, please consider questions such as the following:

- What are the insights I can gain here? What insights do I need to develop?

- What is in plain sight that I can use, leverage, develop or take advantage of?

- What foresight do I need to develop, create or learn about?

I understand what it's like to raise children, to lead people and to be raised by parents, and I see the similarities in these relationships across the many leaders I have worked with throughout my career. When, in a coaching session or workshop I'm running, my clients describe a situation or circumstance with their people, I often reflect on my feelings of déjà vecu (yep, that term again) with what they have described. The likenesses and similarities are many. I have also found that my children perform at their best and want to do the right thing when they:

- have clear structure, boundaries and consequences

- eat well and get lots of exercise

- feel loved and supported, in an environment that is encouraging and caring

- know where they are headed, and how they will get there

- have good role models in their life.

The same applies to those you lead.

How to use this book

What you will find in the following pages are case studies, practical advice and tools to help you become a better leader and create great leaders. I read a lot of business books that have great concepts, theories and ideas, yet I'm left to try to figure out how to implement them. These books lack practical methods you can actually start using. This is not what this book is about. I'm here to support and guide you with pragmatism and common sense – it's what I love doing and what I aim to do within all the work I do with my clients so they get the most value.

I also don't believe in over-complicating anything – in fact, I can't stand complexity. It hurts my brain, and leaves me confused, lost and pissed off. So you won't find anything in here that is confusing. Indeed, the chapters will probably surprise you in their simplicity. Nothing is in here that you haven't heard about before in some way, shape or form – because the information is logical and common sense, which is what seems to be missing in so very many things these days!

In the first two chapters of this book, I describe the challenges that leaders face today, what we have become as a society and how this affects the way we lead our people and raise our children. I also consider how inclusive we actually are as a society, the stress this lack of inclusiveness causes, and how we are losing the attributes of leadership that our people are looking for and that our customers want. Finally, I outline the similarities between raising children and leading people, and introduce you to my five core leadership principles: Love, Environment, Health, Language and Vision.

In chapters 3 to 7, I delve into each of my five core principles in more detail, showing how you have already experienced each one, either through your parents or as a parent. I outline how the principles are already being used by leaders or organisations, and include practical steps and techniques to help you implement each one.

The final chapter in the book then considers the broader view of leadership, and the different ways you can assess what you already have with your team, what you already know about your people and what you need to do in the future to create a more cohesive, productive and engaged team.

As English philosopher John Locke said, 'Reading furnishes the mind only with materials of knowledge; it is thinking that makes what we read ours'.

So let's get going and learn about raising leaders, building your knowledge so you can make it yours.

Chapter 1

SIGHTSEEING

As I opened my eyes, I felt the intense sensation that someone had poured a bucket of sand in them while I was asleep.
I looked at my husband, then at the clock. One hour – one
solitary hour had passed since I had gone to bed, exhausted.
He looked at me with sympathy and concern as he told me
that the baby was awake. *Seriously?* I thought. *How can he
have slept for one hour and think that it's now okay to be awake?*
But I dragged my sorry arse out of bed and went to his cot,
where I tried to feed, soothe and comfort – anything to get
him to go back to sleep. My brain was barely functioning,
and feelings of anger, frustration and exhaustion flooded my
mind and body. Isolation, inadequacy and doubt had become
my daily companions. My self-esteem seemed to have ebbed
away, slowly eaten by the feelings of helplessness and frustration. I was completely confused about how I could love a
child so unconditionally yet feel complete and utter despair.

When I was expecting our first child, I knew sleep deprivation was one thing I would need to endure. What I experienced, however, was deeper and darker than anything I'd expected, and led to more frustration and confusion than I had ever felt in my life. For the first 18 months of his life, my son, Harry, didn't sleep much. No matter how much I cajoled, caressed, walked, cradled, drove around and wore a path in my carpet for him, he just wasn't keen on it. He was going to the beat of his own drum and seemed out of anyone's control. No matter who we consulted for help and support, nothing worked.

At the time, I was part of a mothers group, consisting of peers who had all had their children around the same time. I went to early meetings with high hopes that I would be able to talk to other people who were going through the same thing that we were. I was disappointed with my experience. I think I was one of the eldest mothers in the group, which may have influenced how I perceived the other girls, and they seemed quick to form subgroups and cliques I wasn't part of. I gave up going after a month. I couldn't connect with anyone there – perhaps because I looked too desperate or needy, but also because they all appeared to have perfect children, perfect families and perfect lives. They all talked like motherhood was so fulfilling and rewarding. Ugh! It made me want to vomit.

Our friends were also having children at the same time and they also seemed to not understand me when I tried to talk about what we were experiencing. Their children seemed to have no problems sleeping, settling and generally existing. When I tried to explain what was happening, I was met with confusion or blank looks as though I was speaking another language – a language that not one other person on the planet could comprehend. I felt alone. I felt isolated. I felt lost.

And things didn't get much easier. As a toddler, Harry had two speeds: unmanageable and asleep. He was always on the go – at home, at kindergarten, everywhere. We were often told by his carers that he wasn't cooperative, would lash out at the other kids, and wasn't able to transition between activities without disrupting other children or becoming frustrated and angry. We sought the advice of many paediatricians and child psychologists and were provided a list of behaviour management strategies that just never seemed to work. Harry definitely had a mind of his own and didn't want to do anything that we asked him to do if it wasn't also what he wanted to do.

As parents, we both felt restricted in what we could do and where we could take Harry. Any change in environment seemed to bring a whole new set of triggers for his behaviour. He could be set off into a fit of rage in what seemed like the blink of an eye and often without a foreseeable trigger. While our friends were taking their kids out everywhere, including overseas, we felt confined to a set environment trying to keep things consistent, constrained and limited.

If parenting were a paid job, at the time I probably would have been on performance management. I couldn't get my son to do anything for me or be compliant with what I wanted him to do – at best, he would say, 'Yes, Mummy, okay' and then do the exact opposite. I couldn't negotiate, influence, cajole, persuade, entice, sweet-talk or coax him to do anything he didn't want to do. My confidence was diminishing daily and I couldn't see a way forward or out of what I was living. No matter what I did, nothing seemed to get any better, and I started to question my abilities.

These feelings of self-doubt and frustration can also be experienced by leaders in the workplace. As a leader, you can find it difficult to get your people to own their work, be accountable for what they are doing and follow through on what they have agreed to. They may work with some team members and not others, rarely collaborate or share knowledge with each other, and some may actively work to sabotage you and your department. They can be difficult, temperamental, needy, uncaring, unsociable and downright nasty at times. On top of this, adequate help and support doesn't seem to be available, no-one understands what you're experiencing and any strategies you are given seem to be useless. Yes, leading a team is like raising children.

Both roles can be blindingly frustrating. As a parent or leader, you can sometimes resort to strategies like yelling and scolding your people – and then packing your bags for the guilt trip you're about to take. Or you try to negotiate an outcome with them and end up with a deal that is nowhere near what you wanted, yet somehow you've been made to think you're the winner (until you discover you've been conned). Or it's an arm wrestle won by whoever has the stronger will for getting their own way, again resulting in the guilt trip or the threat of having the sugar police on your doorstep – because, say, you gave your child chocolate to get in the car because they were refusing to do anything when you needed to get out the door to an important meeting, the outcome of which would result in either the downfall of humanity or making your boss an obscene amount of money, which you would receive no actual acknowledgement or return for because you missed buying company shares because your toddler vomited on the application form and you were too embarrassed to return it. Sigh!

Like me with my mothers group, you no doubt also compare yourself to your peers and this can make you feel inadequate, underperforming or incompetent as a leader, parent or both. Every other parent has the perfect home, perfect partner and perfect children who always behave, do as they're told instantly and have little halos floating around above their head, along with big smiles that sparkle and glint. Basically, everyone else's children are well-mannered, polite little bunnies just like in the movies! And every other leader at your work and beyond has the perfect team, achieves all of their goals, leads people who collaborate and innovate and is the boss's favourite employee. You have no actual evidence of this, but know it to be true – so there! You end up hating your job, your peers, your team and yourself. You feel like you get no support from anyone, everyone from the CEO to the cleaner seems to be working against you, and everything you do is never quite right or good enough. Leadership, like parenting, is lonely, hard and often thankless.

What have we become?

If you live a life of frustration in an environment that is unaccountable, unsupportive and uncollaborative, your stress levels will increase considerably. When you're constantly stressed, you face higher potential for illness, disease or an early death. According to the Australian Bureau of Statistics

(ABS) 2018 National Health Survey, approximately one in eight people, or 2.4 million Australians, experienced 'high or very high levels of psychological distress', influenced in no small way by work. When you are under stress, your body produces hormones such as cortisol and adrenaline, which increase your blood pressure, causing hypertension. Also according to the ABS, approximately one in ten Australians, or 2.6 million people, report having hypertension or high blood pressure, with the proportion of people aged between 35 and 44 with hypertension having tripled since 2014–15.

We are also becoming a society that is less tolerant and more critical of each other. We have become very opinionated, unsympathetic and intolerant of each other's views and opinions. We call out other people – for their biases, views, opinions, dress sense, friendships, personality flaws, food preferences, social standing, social media opinions, social justice choices (and the list goes on), along with the important issues of racism, homophobia, bigotry and misogyny – at every opportunity, for even the smallest indiscretion. Don't get me wrong – I believe that racism, homophobia, bigotry and misogyny must be called out at every opportunity. However, when we are calling out every other useless thing – which usually just comes down to personal opinion – calling out the bad things gets lost in the noise of the trivial stuff. When everything is important, nothing is important, and we waste time and energy on the rubbish at the expense of the important messages. Sadly, I also think the reason for calling out the small stuff is some kind of need to feel better about ourselves or to look and feel more self-righteous. In its current form, I think this is plainly and simply bullying, and it needs to stop.

In a 2016 study completed by Robin Kowalski, Allison Toth and Megan Morgan on bullying and cyberbullying in adulthood and the workplace, they found that 20 per cent of respondents had been bullied or cyberbullied as an adult, with 30 per cent being bullied at work. Similarly, a 2014 study on online harassment by the Pew Research Center found that '73% of adult internet users have seen someone be harassed in some way online and 40% have personally experienced it'. The American Osteopathic Association has highlighted that online bullying can lead to sleep loss, headaches, muscle pain, anxiety and depression, and, according to a Norwegian study published in the *American Journal of Public Health* in 2015, online bullying has also been identified as a precursor to suicidal thinking. We condemn bullying in its physical form, yet we seem to accept it in its online form. I find this appalling and frightening.

In his December 2019 speech to shareholders, the chairman of Orica, Malcolm Broomhead, commented:

> *It's a great shame that 30 years after the fall of the Berlin Wall, where there was great hope of a future united world, we seem to just be pulling ourselves apart in a frenzy of self-righteousness. And there's an attitude of 'I'm right and I'll shout down anyone who disagrees', and it's becoming increasingly prevalent.*

This type of behaviour is dividing our world more than ever, reducing empathy and compassion while increasing judgement and unacceptance. If we continue to do this, the future for our children frightens me.

Opening our eyes

I often hear organisations espouse their values of diversity and inclusion. Yet, to truly be an inclusive society, we need to be less judgemental and accept everyone for their views, acknowledge their entitlement to them and live and let live beside them. In his book *Leadership in the Age of Personalization: Why standardization fails in the age of 'me'*, Glenn Llopis cites his survey of more than 14,000 leaders and their employees at a broad range of companies across the US, highlighting that the number-one thing employees wanted in order to be their authentic self at work was 'a safe environment where no-one is judged'. This was twice as important as 'feeling valued and respected' and having 'trust and transparency from their supervisor'. It's incredible that we want this at work, we want this for our children, yet we find it incredibly difficult to actually live it.

So, how do we start to live in a world where we accept others openly, we create connection and we become someone that others aspire to be like? Let's start with comparison. When I compared myself to the other mothers in my mothers group, I felt inferior, like I wasn't coping and that everyone had it easier than I did. The fourth rule in Jordan Peterson's book *12 Rules for Life: An antidote to chaos* is, 'Compare yourself to who you were yesterday, not to who someone else is today'. In this rule, he talks about making small changes to yourself and your circumstances each day, every day until they're incorporated into your life. Then stand back and look at how far you have come. Comparing yourself to the person you were at the start of these changes to who you are sometime later is more rewarding and relevant than comparing yourself to someone else.

When you make small changes to the way you are, the things you say, how you behave and what you do, these add up to significant changes over time. Through focused effort on small improvements we can actually impact more broadly on our world.

Now let's consider kindness, compassion and empathy for others. Where have these gone? It's like we have suddenly woken up devoid of these emotions. These are such valuable commodities in leadership, yet we've become a society of hard-arse, judgemental and inconsiderate pricks. Yet the value of these attributes to organisations is evident. In a *Harvard Business Review* study of 84 US companies focusing on the level of compassion and forgiveness held by the CEOs, researchers found companies with a CEO who had higher levels of these characteristics outperformed their peers by almost 500 per cent.

Additionally, Audun Farbrot for the BI Norwegian Business School researched 1500 leaders and their employees and found that leaders who show good self-insight, are humble and good role models for their people 'are rewarded with committed and service-minded employees'. The self-insight Farbrot refers to means these leaders had a strong understanding of their emotions, behaviours, abilities and needs, and when faced with challenges, they are proactive rather than reactive.

Sightseeing

Intellectual excellence owes its birth and growth mainly to instruction, and so requires time and experience, while moral excellence is the result of habit or custom.
Aristotle

Creating *insight* into the things we do and say is the first place to start to create a better world for our children, as well as those we lead. Reflection should become a part of your daily routine, a habit built around understanding what you do and what you can learn from it. Evidence suggests that the habit of reflection can lead to increases in wellbeing, productivity and meaning in our lives. In a 2015 article published in the *Journal of Organizational Behavior*, Laurenz Meier, Eunae Cho and Soner Dumani found a correlation between reflection and increased wellbeing and mood. Additionally, research conducted by Giada Di Stefano, Gary Pisano, Francesca Gino and Bradley Staats for the Harvard Business School found that daily reflection of just 15 minutes can increase performance by up to 23 per cent.

We can also learn about our people through understanding their stories, in turn strengthening the trust and connection we have in our relationships with them. And, according to 'The Neuroscience of Trust' by Paul Zak (published in the *Harvard Business Review*), when we have strong foundations of trust in our teams and organisations, we see increases to productivity, energy and engagement, and decreased stress levels, sick days and burnout. Through this insight, you are able to influence the health, wellbeing and mindset of your people and ensure you practise good work–life balance for the benefit of the team.

When you see what's in *plain sight* of you and within your control, you become self-sufficient, resilient and empowered. Your words, actions and behaviours are the only things that you can control and once you start to focus on that, instead of on what you can't control, your world becomes larger. In Stephen Covey's best-selling book *The 7 Habits of Highly Effective People*, he talks about your circle of influence and circle of concern and how, if you focus on the things you have influence on – for example, your own self – you find that your circle of influence grows. Additionally, having a proactive focus leads to positive energy, which also enlarges your circle of influence. So, when we are proactive in establishing boundaries and expectations and create a culture of accountability for our people to operate in, we build autonomous, independent and empowered teams.

And when we have the *foresight* to understand the true purpose of the work we do, and the vision and strategy to build a better world, we inspire the people we lead. Research completed by PricewaterhouseCoopers (and included in their report 'Putting Purpose to Work: A study of purpose in the workplace', released in 2016) found that almost 80 per cent of leaders believe that their purpose is fundamental to their success. Additionally, a survey completed by Sean Czarnecki in 2018 found that consumers are more loyal to brands that are purpose driven and believe them to be more caring.

It is critical to your business to engage your people in the process of developing your strategy, so they can find and connect with your purpose to make their work meaningful, and clearly understand your vision of where you want to go. Until you have all three, you run the risk of not achieving what you set out to. As Bill Cushard highlights, studies show only 14 per cent of your employees understand your organisation strategy and only 41 per cent understand its overall direction. (For more information in this area, see also articles by Donald Sull, Stefano Turconi, Charles Sull, and James Yoder, published in 2017, and David Witt, published in 2012.) If this is the case, your odds of achieving anything are significantly reduced. Investing the time and effort into helping every single employee understand your vision, strategy and purpose will reap your organisation rewards in the long term.

Through creating insight, looking at what's in plain sight and having foresight, you are able to develop and adapt to what needs to be done, build the confidence in yourself and your people to build something incredible together, and become a successful, high-performing and empowered team of people through understanding, empathy, connection and trust. Learning and adapting throughout your leadership journey is key to becoming a leader who people respect, are inspired by and want to work for. It's what leadership is all about.

> *The pessimist complains about the wind. The optimist expects it to change. The leader adjusts the sails.*
>
> **John Maxwell,** author and speaker
> (also attributed to William Arthur Ward)

Something to think about

The last few months of 2019 saw a number of instances in the media where people were criticised, chastised and bullied for not having the same views, beliefs or behaviours that others believed they should. For example, American comedian and talk show host Ellen DeGeneres being friends with former American President George Bush was seen by some as inconceivable, given the two have such opposing beliefs. To some, it's clearly not possible for two people to be mature enough to acknowledge each other's views and opinions are opposite yet still be able to look past that to who the other person actually is. Having the respect to say to each other that they will agree to disagree, and keep open the possibility that one day, one of them may even change their mind about how they currently see something, seems an impossible concept to some.

Other examples include people's reactions to rugby union player Israel Folau's homophobia and his views on gay marriage, climate activist Greta Thunberg's address to the United Nations and Australian underworld crime figure Mick Gatto working with The Salvation Army to help the homeless on World Homeless Day. To some, this final example is abhorrent given the disparate beliefs of each party and, well, Mick couldn't possibly care about the homeless, could he?

I often come across people who are fearful of putting forth their views because of being misinterpreted, judged or labelled something terrible, so they remain quiet and keep their thoughts and views to themselves. Creating a safe work environment is a key skill for leaders, and one that encourages this diversity of thinking and a tolerance of inclusiveness to come about. Hate speech, homophobia, sexism and racism are never okay. But the conversation needs to continue, rather than forcing people further into their opposing corners. True inclusiveness is having the courage to accept people for what they are, how they behave and what they think, regardless of whether we agree or not. It's the ability to agree to disagree, but to keep talking, accepting others from all sides of faith, religion, sexuality, beliefs, values, thoughts and opinions, and forgiving even if it's hard to do.

> *We could learn a lot from crayons; some are sharp, some are pretty, some are dull, while others bright, some have weird names, but they all have learned to live together in the same box.*
>
> **Robert Fulghum**, author and minister

Ways to improve your sightseeing

- Consider your own childhood experience with your parents. How has this influenced the way you lead? Are you transferring anything onto those you work with?

- Reflecting on your last year, month or day, what are the things that you thought went well? What things didn't go well?

- When you think about the things that went well or didn't go well, what about the situation did or didn't work? What about your responses did or didn't work? What was your mindset like at the time?

- If you are a parent, what similarities can you see between raising your kids and leading your people? What can you learn from this? How can you use similar strategies?

- Are you taking on the role of mother/father/sister/ brother with any of your people? Is it working? Can you change the way you respond?

- Are you comparing yourself to others and feeling like you're coming up short? When you think about what you were doing five years ago and what you are doing now, do you see a different comparison?

Chapter 2

LIFE IMITATING LEADERSHIP

It's fair to say that Queen Elizabeth II had a difficult time throughout 2019. A number of controversies rocked the royal family during this time, starting with the Duke of Edinburgh's car accident (where a woman was injured after the Duke hit her car with his Land Rover). Later in the year, it was reported that the Queen's granddaughter Zara Tindall received large sums of money from a Hong Kong businessman in return for introductions to the royal family. And in October, Harry and Meghan, Duke and Duchess of Sussex, launched legal action against *The Mail on Sunday* for reporting 'false' and 'deliberately derogatory' stories regarding the Duchess. Many articles also focused on the supposed rift between Harry and his brother William, Duke of Cambridge, and the rift between their wives Catherine and Meghan. We were then all privy to the train wreck interview of Prince Andrew, Duke of York, regarding his relationship with American businessman Jeffrey Epstein. And, at the start of 2020, we witnessed the fallout from Harry and Meghan's announcement that they would step back from their roles as senior members of the royal family, preferring to spend their time between the UK and Canada and to earn their own way in life. That's a lot for any parent to bear, queen or otherwise, and for it to play out in the very public domain of the press makes it even harder.

The Queen, as the leader of the Commonwealth, has shown great leadership over the years, displaying a commitment to her duty and the Commonwealth. From a very early age, it was clear she took her role in the royal family seriously. Born on 21 April 1926 in London, Princess Elizabeth was not expected to become the monarch. However, after the abdication of her uncle, King Edward, in 1936, she became second in line to the throne. At the age of 14, Elizabeth gave her first speech, reassuring the evacuated children during the Second World War. In 1945, Elizabeth joined the Auxiliary Territorial Service and became an expert driver and mechanic alongside other British women. When her father was made king, in preparation for her future role as queen, she studied constitutional history and law and also received lessons in religion from the Archbishop of Canterbury. Following the death of her father, King George VI, in 1952, Elizabeth was crowned Queen Elizabeth II on 2 June 1953 at the age of 27.

She has also shown the ability to adapt and embrace change throughout her career – for example, by insisting that her coronation be televised, against the advice of then Prime

Minister Winston Churchill, so that people could feel more involved with the event. Queen Elizabeth also adopted new technology, being one of the first heads of state to send an email on 26 March 1976 as part of a demonstration of new technology by the Royal Signals and Radar Establishment (RSRE).

Elizabeth has lived through a great deal in her lifetime – including a world war and civil wars, such as in the Falklands and Iraq; an assassination attempt in 1981 during a trip to New Zealand, when a shot was fired at her car; changes in society as it moved from a primarily Christian society to a diverse, multicultural one; terrorist attacks in London over the last 20 years; and her children's divorces and personal lives paraded through the media. Without exception, she has managed everything that comes at her with the courage, spirit and dignity of a great leader. (See the references provided at the end of this book for the sources of this information, including Biography.com, Computer History Museum, *Newsweek* and *Time* magazine.)

Without doubt, the hardest challenges the Queen has ever had to endure have been to do with her family. Each time, using the same principles for both family and work has held her in good stead. As a mother who loves her children, she would undoubtedly be heartbroken by the behaviour of her son Andrew and her grandchildren Zara and Harry. Yet her love for her family helps her to make the sometimes difficult decisions she has had to make and show a level of tough love when required. She is acutely aware of the delicate balancing act between her stakeholders and the 'firm', and that her behaviours are in the spotlight and she must set a good example for those watching. Prince William once summed up the Monarchy as, 'It's about setting examples. It's about doing one's duty as she would say. It's about using your position for the good'. (Quoted in 'Duty is the key to the Queen's success', published in *Newsweek*.) The Queen also listens, asks questions, observes and considers before making any decision, keeping her mind razor sharp. She has a vision, values and a sense of purpose that have guided her throughout the good and bad times. (For more on this, see the *Newsweek* article and Muneeb Siddiqui's 2019 article.)

The interesting thing about life is that it gives us wonderful opportunities to practise great leadership, and none greater than in having the privilege of raising children.

If you look, you can see similarities between leadership and parenting

If you look around you, you will see many examples of the similarities between leadership and parenting. For example, when Jacinda Ardern, Prime Minister of New Zealand, was faced with a country grieving the actions of a lone terrorist who killed 50 people, her compassion and empathy for her people mimicked those of any mother or father for their children if they experience trauma and loss. In 2010, President Barack Obama, 44th President of the United States, signed the *Healthy, Hunger-Free Kids Act* to fund nutrition and free lunch programs in schools, caring for the health and well-being of children as he does his own. Sister Norma Pimentel runs a Humanitarian Respite Center in Texas where she helps new migrants to the US to 'catch their breath' with a meal, shower, clothing and travel assistance, showing the compassion and care of any parent. And Walmart executives Doug McMillon and Lisa Woods launched the Centers for Excellence program to provide their 1.5 million employees with affordable hospital procedures at a significantly reduced cost, showing the priority they place on the health and wellbeing of their people.

Common areas of the parenting and leadership experience

You don't need to be a parent to be able to see the comparisons. We have all been raised by someone – parent or carer – who (hopefully) showed the actions and consideration parents are known for. When you observe the leadership behaviours of those leaders you admire, you will see similarities with your own experience. Like parenting, leadership is difficult, challenging and rewarding, sometimes all in the first hour of the day. Whether parenting or leading, you need to focus on my five core leadership areas to get the best out of your people. These core areas are shown in figure 2.1 on the next page, and the following sections introduce them in more detail.

Figure 2.1: Core areas of leadership

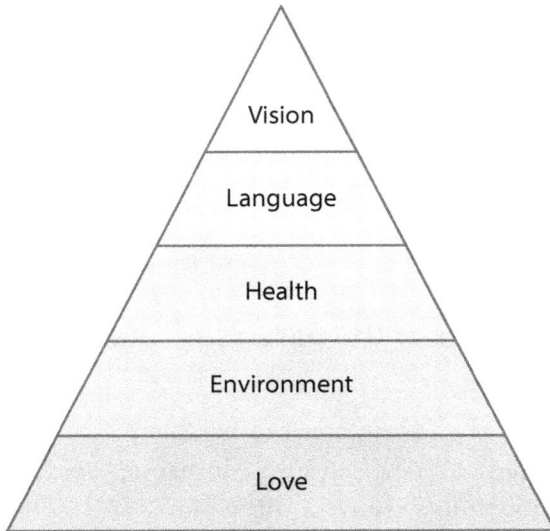

Love

> *Leaders touch a heart before they ask for a hand.*
> **John Maxwell**, author and speaker

At the foundation of any family is love and so too must this exist at the foundation of teams. Through connection, understanding and forgiveness, you can build a strong, cohesive team that understands and values each member's knowledge and skills. It will enable you to engage in the same types of arguments you have at Christmas time with your family after lunch, and has an increased commitment to the success of the team as a whole, similar to the indebtedness you have for the sacrifices your parents made when raising you and your siblings. Through finding the similarities we have with each other and learning to appreciate our differences, whether we agree with them or not, we can form truly inclusive teams, organisations, communities and societies.

After a longitudinal study completed in 2014 and outlined in the article 'What's love got to do with it?', researchers concluded that organisations that have a culture of companionate love between employees have significantly higher levels of engagement and lower levels of withdrawal (emotional exhaustion and absenteeism). They also found that this permeates out to clients, customers and stakeholders. When there is a culture that supports connection, care, compassion and empathy, employees are happier, more dedicated and satisfied with their work. Love really does have a lot to do with it.

Environment

In all good homes, creating an environment for children to grow and thrive is essential in setting them up for success. So too is the environment you create for the people you lead. Creating the psychological safety for your people to feel free to express themselves in whatever way they require will help to foster the creativity and innovation your organisation needs to continue to be successful and relevant in its market. As a parent or leader, you also need to set clear expectations and consequences for your people so they understand what work needs to be done and by when, and the consequences if the work is not completed. This creates an environment of accountability and performance. This environment also encourages robust debate and enables people to feel comfortable to voice their views and opinions without fear of being judged and excluded.

The Gallup Q12 survey used 12 items that link to strong business outcomes. The results from this, published in 2015, highlighted that when employees have clear expectations and the resources to do their job, engagement increases dramatically. Additionally, research completed by Amy Edmondson and Zhike Lei in 2014 for Harvard Business School found that organisations that create psychologically safe environments for their people have increased innovation and desire to improve their team or organisation. Yet, the Australian Workplace Psychological Safety Survey, completed in 2017, found that 56 per cent of employees agreed with the statement, 'If you make a mistake at work, it is often held against you'. The survey also found that only 34 per cent of respondents felt safe to take risks at work and 58 per cent of people felt their colleagues rejected those who were different. We have an obligation to create a safe environment for our people, setting concise expectations and clear consequences, before we can truly claim we are inclusive.

Health

We want our children to be able to thrive in a world that is increasingly demanding and where stress is at an all-time high. When they are healthy and happy, both physically and mentally, they create the skills and resilience to be able to meet these demands. The same applies to the people who work for you. By supporting your people to create balance and boundaries between work and home, live healthy lives through diet and exercise and have a positive mindset to be able to approach their work and challenges with the resilience needed, you will help your team to manage stress, reduce illness and increase their engagement. Research completed by Ron Friedman in 2014, and J.C. Coulson, Jim McKenna and M. Field in 2008, and further research highlighted by Barry Chignell in 2018, all suggests that healthy cultures also create healthy relationships with peers, stakeholders and customers, increase our ability to assess risk and make better decisions, increase productivity and reduce errors.

A 2018 survey completed in the US by the National Business Group on Health found that:

> *Employees are looking to their employer to provide support on all areas of well-being – not just physical health programs focused on losing weight or understanding health risks – but those designed to help employees meet their financial, mental, community and social health goals.*

Organisations have an opportunity to support their people more in this domain, because the up- and downstream benefits are clear.

Language

It's confronting when your child repeats back to you the same words, phrases or slang that you know you use every day. It's particularly horrifying when the words used are a cuss at some other driver, or, you make an error and your child chastises you with your own words. As parents, we are constantly on show, being watched and observed, listened to (even though it often appears otherwise) and teaching our children how to behave. The exact same things happen when we lead people. They watch, observe and take in all of our words, actions, behaviours and values, good and bad. As Stephen Covey says, 'What you do has far greater impact than what you say'. This means that having the emotional intelligence to be able to reflect on and understand what you do, make modifications and learn from your mistakes creates the same awareness in your people. It also says that you're not perfect and you should continue to learn from your mistakes so you don't do the same thing in the future.

Research completed by Carmen Tanner, Adrian Brügger, Susan van Schie and Carmen Lebherz in 2010 shows a positive relationship between a leader's ethical behaviours and the attitudes of employees to their jobs. Attitudes such as job satisfaction, commitment to the organisation and overall engagement were all positively influenced by the actions of their leader. It's like yawning when someone else yawns: we can't help it. According to Sara Miller (in 'Here's why yawns are so contagious'), scientists tell us the reaction is an 'echophenomenon' or an 'automatic imitation of another person'. So, if it's that easy to influence the way your people behave, surely it's worth taking a look at how you behave.

Vision

We all have hopes and dreams for our children – usually focusing on them growing up and being successful at whatever they choose to do, and being happy with their life, partner, job, dreams and aspirations. As a leader, you also want your people to do well, and to thrive, develop, learn and succeed. It's important to have a vision of the future and a strategy for how to get there, both personally and professionally. Having vision and strategy helps your people to make a link between what they do on a daily basis and the goals of the team and organisation. Understanding the purpose underlying the vision also creates meaning in the work they do and a connection with each other, their team and the organisation.

> *The purpose of life is not to be happy – but to matter, to be productive, to be useful, to have it make some difference that you lived at all.*
> **Leo Rosten**, author and political scientist

Walt Disney's first job was a cartoonist at *The Kansas City Star* newspaper, which he was fired from in 1919 because he 'lacked imagination and good ideas'. Oprah Winfrey was fired from a job as an evening news reporter because she was 'unfit for television'. Steven Spielberg was rejected from film school three times. All three went on to achieve amazing accomplishments because they had a clear purpose, strategy and a defining vision of where they wanted to go. Instead of stopping there, they all went on to become incredible achievers, pushing through the obstacles they faced because they strongly believed in what they wanted to achieve. Their vision provided them with the focus and perseverance required to accomplish the significant goals they set for themselves.

Five levels of development

When we think about the similarities between parenting and leadership, we are also able to determine the five levels of development that we go through in our careers and how they apply to the people whom we lead.

As your people move through each development level, their value increases to the team and organisation, and they strengthen and develop their own leadership skills along the way. Each level has an impact on your team and their progress and, as with your children when they are at different stages in life, being able to manage each as they grow and develop helps them to progress and create the skills and gain the experience they need to become adults. Each stage requires your guidance, support and direction to facilitate growth and evolution.

The following table outlines these five levels, and the following sections provide more detail, including how each level relates to the people you lead.

Level	Stage	Result	Value
5	Adult	You're in control, leading the way, kicking goals	+100
4	Teenager	You're taking risks, being independent, finding your own way	+50
3	Child	You're becoming independent, with direction	0
2	Toddler	You're finding your way, with guidance	-50
1	Baby	You're dependent, unsure, fearful	-100

Level 1: Baby

At this stage, your people are dependent, unsure of themselves and requiring lots of guidance and support to achieve what they need to. They are often fearful and will come to you to provide the answers to the challenges they face. They need help to focus on the things that matter and will be drawn into the detail, needing guidance to see the strategic and how this links to the operational. They are also learning to communicate effectively with others and to follow simple instructions.

Level 2: Toddler

Prone to emotional outbursts, toddlers are beginning to learn about emotional intelligence. They are also learning to collaborate with others and will need lots of encouragement to do so. They will require your guidance and support to understand the feelings of others as they learn to navigate their way through work. Learning occurs through mistakes and errors, so an environment of psychological safety is critical to help them through. This is a big learning stage as they find their way in the world of work.

Level 3: Child

Becoming more independent and learning about their influence on others defines the 'child' level. While still learning, people at this level are definitely coming into their own and willing to take more risks, knowing you are there to support them if they fail. Their communication skills are developing in a more refined way; however, they need support and guidance to develop their empathy and compassion for others. They are more self-sufficient and starting to move into uncharted territory.

Level 4: Teenager

People at 'teenager' level are very independent and want more responsibility, so you will be able to step back more and give them some latitude to make their own decisions. They will come to you for guidance if they really can't figure things out, so your role should shift from supervisor to mentor to enable their skills in problem-solving to flourish. Providing guidance through other senior leaders will help them to develop a more balanced perspective, as well as increase their networks and brand.

Level 5: Adult

Adults are in control, self-sufficient and leading their own people, and are confident, self-assured and comfortable with their own leadership style. They are your next in line and look to you as a trusted mentor, knowing you have their best interests at heart and trust them to deliver to a high standard. They are taking on more and more leadership, across more boundaries, and have highly developed emotional intelligence. They role model the right words, actions and behaviours and are leaders of leaders.

So, where do you see your people now, and where would you like them to be?

Levelling up

Like most leaders, you want to develop your team to be self-sufficient, emotionally intelligent and leading the way in the organisation you work for. You want them all to be adults, so you can shift your focus to being a leader who is there for trusted guidance and support, safe in the knowledge that your team will deliver what they say they will, on time and in an adult manner.

Like Queen Elizabeth with her children, you know your team will let you down at some stage and to some degree; however, you have the professionalism and years of experience to know how to support them, forgive them and help them to learn from their mistakes. You will be able to make the tough decisions, take a firm line if needed, and help them to move through in the best way possible.

Like parenting, leadership is a journey for you and your team, with everyone learning, evolving and growing at different paces.

You're creating your work family – where people look out for each other, argue constructively, can agree to disagree with each other, accept the final call with good grace and dignity, support each other through good times and bad, and know someone has their back when they are in trouble. It sounds like a great team to work in.

When you're leading this team you will feel like a proud parent, having been the creator of something special, which people will talk about for a long time and others will look to as an example of great leadership.

Something to think about

Richard Branson, billionaire and founder of the Virgin Group, a parent to daughter, Holly, and son, Sam, and grandparent to five, believes that raising children is just as tough and equally as rewarding as running a business and leading people. As he noted in his 2019 blog post, 'The business of being a parent (and grand-dude)', from starting a new business through to running an empire, the similarities between business and parenting are many.

Branson believes that having a new baby is like starting a new business. You are seldom prepared for what really happens, even though you put in many hours of planning ahead of the day. For example, on the day his daughter was born his wife had to kick him out of bed, 'worse for wear' from a Virgin party the day before. Also, at the launch of Virgin Trains in the US, he notes, he was almost killed when a banner came crashing down above him. No matter how prepared you think you are, things can always go wrong.

He also believes that you need to get involved in the work that your people do. He uses the metaphor of changing a baby's nappy in the blog post, and that you don't know how to do it until you try it. The same applies to many aspects of running a business, in that you sometimes need to get your hands dirty doing the work and the best way to learn is through doing it alongside your people.

And, finally, Branson believes that at times you need to take a step back and let your people shine, as you do with your children as they grow up. He is rarely closely involved with the CEO and leadership teams of his businesses, so that they have the freedom to learn, grow and fail. This allows him to also take time out to appreciate what he has achieved, look at the big picture and think about what's next.

Ways to make connections between parenting and leading

- Consider a period when you went through hard times, either as a parent or with your parents. Was the situation dealt with using love and compassion? What leadership skills can you learn from this experience?

- Think about a time when your parents forgave you for something you did. How did it feel to know you had their support? Have you been forgiven for doing something – or forgiven someone – at work?

- How have you responded to your parents' expectations about your life? Was it beneficial to have clear expectations and consequences to guide you?

- How does the health and wellbeing of your kids affect their thoughts and behaviours? Do you see similarities in those you work with or lead?

- Have you seen one of your relatives say something and then do the opposite? What about someone at work?

- What do you envisage for the future of your children? Do you have a vision for your team or organisation?

- Can you see how either you or your children have passed through the five levels of development? Where are your team members in their development?

Chapter 3

THE 'L' WORD –
WHAT YOU BRING

At the age of six, Gerald (not his real name) was expelled from Prep, his first year of school. The school was a private school with a tag line that professed they knew boys and how to teach them. Disappointingly, they failed in his case. Gerald had always had difficulty transitioning between activities, from the time that he had commenced in any kind of childcare. His parents had raised this with his teachers on many occasions, but when they received a phone call to say that Gerald had not wanted to finish an activity with paper and scissors, became upset and then allegedly threatened the teacher with said scissors, they were politely asked to leave. They were never allowed to speak to the teacher concerned to fully understand the situation so it's difficult to truly know how it all transpired. And, of course, disarming a six-year-old of a school-issued pair of scissors was apparently out of the question.

After a short period at a school for children with behavioural issues, Gerald moved to a state school. Here, he had a short-lived period of stability before he again started to become disruptive, aggressive and uncontrollable. To their credit, the school did a great deal to try to manage Gerald's school life, at one stage breaking his day down into 15-minute increments of activities to ensure he wouldn't get bored. Unfortunately, this didn't produce the required results and, after many meetings and an incident with another sharp object and a teacher, Gerald was once again asked to leave. Thankfully, again, no-one was harmed.

The next school was designed for kids with behaviour issues. This school had many rules, with good behaviour rewarded through a system of points that the kids earned or lost. After about six months, Gerald was moved onto a different reward program, similar to a traffic light system – if his behaviours progressed to a red status, for example, he would be required to be collected for the day. After three strikes, he would be asked to leave the school. They left the school.

During this time, Gerald's behaviour at home was erratic. He would get very angry and sometimes violent if he was told he couldn't have something, or his parents tried to implement consequences for poor behaviour. They tried all manner of behaviour management strategies, including limiting time on iPad and computer games – at which point, he would become violent, almost explosive and lash out. Both parents received black eyes during this time, and his mother had many cuts and bruises and at times wondered if she was receiving a form of domestic violence. It was a tough experience for everyone in the family.

Support was available, and it came through the full breadth and depth of paediatricians, child psychologists, occupational therapists and counsellors – each one with a diagnosis, therapy, medication and professional opinion. Nothing seemed to work, and Gerald's parents felt like no-one could actually understand what it was really like for them. Everyone had thoughts, opinions and advice to give, but again, nothing ever seemed to work. It was isolating and his parents felt alone, frustrated and worried. In one instance, a counsellor commented on how good they were for enduring so much, and they thought, *He's our child, of course we're going to stay the course.* It was a very difficult time for everyone, but not once did their love for Gerald waver. You don't always like your children, but your love for them endures anything.

What's love got to do with it?

Love is at the very foundation of families, and without love I doubt that civilisation would still exist. It's at the heart of every moment that our kids do things that surprise and delight us, and equally at each time we are disappointed and heartbroken by them. We don't give up on our kids, no matter how often they do things that are wrong or take advantage of us, because we have a connection with them. They make us feel vulnerable and, as parents, our job is to guide them successfully through life. 'But what's love got to do with the workplace?' I hear you ask. This is a business book, after all. Surely, I don't think that you need to love the people you lead? Yep, that's exactly what I'm saying.

According to the Ancient Greeks, love comes in eight different types: *agape* (unconditional love), *eros* (erotic love), *philia* (affectionate love without physical attraction), *storge* (the love we have for family), *ludus* (playful love, such as flirting, new love), *mania* (obsessive love), *pragma* (enduring love that has developed and matured over time) and *philautia* (self-love, including compassion for self and self-esteem). So, when I talk about love in the workplace I specifically mean *philia* and *pragma*, not *eros* (which everyone seems to start with and some among us seem to want to go with). Love in the workplace is about having a connection with people, developing respect and trust between each other and being able to be vulnerable together.

Vince Lombardi, the head coach of the Green Bay Packers American Football team, was a tough man who liked to repeat fellow coach Red Sanders' quote that, 'Winning isn't everything. It's the only thing'. Lombardi was renowned for being one of the greatest coaches in the industry and in the 1960s led his team to three straight NFL Championships. He has also been quoted as saying:

> *I don't necessarily have to like my players and associates but as their leader I* must *love them. Love is loyalty, love is teamwork, love respects the dignity of the individual. This is the strength of any organization.*

Creating this type of love in our teams and organisations enables our people to please and delight us, as well as disappoint and let us down in a kind of similar safety we afford our children. It creates acceptance for the way people are in a non-judgemental environment. It's critical as a foundation.

Creating connections

As humans, we need to connect as much as we need food, water and shelter. Indeed, in *Social: Why our brains are wired to connect*, UCLA Professor Matthew Lieberman says our need to connect has been in our DNA for centuries and is the reason we build tribes, families and communities. This connection makes us feel part of something bigger than just our self and it makes us feel wanted and included. Neurologically, we produce hormones such as oxytocin, a peptide hormone produced by the hypothalamus and released by the posterior pituitary gland that plays a role in social bonding. Our brains also produce dopamine, a chemical of the catecholamine and phenethylamine families responsible for helping us to feel we have done a great job and increasing motivation.

As part of my research for writing this book, I spent some time in the classrooms of my children. This was really enlightening in many ways. One aspect I noted in particular was how the teachers tried very hard to create a connection with the kids. When they had this connection, the children wanted to do great work because it pleased the teachers. The discretionary effort of the children was increased. This doesn't just work with children. A study completed in 2012 by Towers Watson of 32,000 employees across 32 countries found that 'no single behavior more viscerally and reliably influences the quality of people's energy [to do work] than feeling valued and appreciated by their supervisor'.

Yet, we have somehow lost the ability to create this connection, or we create connection with those who are more like us and don't bother with those people we believe aren't like us. It's normal that we are attracted to those people who come into our lives who we believe are like us. When we meet a new person and we 'instantly' connect with them, it's usually because we have quickly determined that we have things in common, we think the same way and we are on the same 'wavelength'. Our brains are naturally attracted to those people we identify as having things in common with us, because when we have commonality, our brain tells us that this person is 'just like me' so they can be trusted. When we have trust, we have connection.

It stands to reason, then, that those people who don't think like you, or you have nothing in common with, or have some strange and exotic views on things mustn't be liked, accepted or trusted. You don't need to look far to find examples of this – they're in the media every day. One notable example was when rugby union star Israel Folau tweeted something the rest of society realised they didn't believe in, but only when placed in the position of having to hear his view. I suspect that many people in Australia wouldn't really have contemplated whether gay people would actually get into heaven or not until Folau's homophobia was plastered all over the news. People were forced to think about what their views were on this and then determine that they didn't actually agree with him – so he is now considered untrustworthy, wrong and discredited in every way possible.

Again, homophobia cannot be tolerated. But does that need to be where the conversation ends? I wonder, if a child came home and said they believed gay people wouldn't get into heaven, whether a parent would cast them out of the house, label them a homophobic and never speak to them again. More likely, the parent would take the time to sit and discuss why they had these views and civilly discuss, debate and perhaps even agree to disagree on the topic for the time being, and then move on with their day. They would continue to accept their child because they have a connection and love them, so they take the time to understand their views with empathy.

Given we afford our children the luxury of understanding and forgiveness, why can't we offer the same privilege to those we lead or work with?

Using the ASK matrix

What if we could find a connection with everyone, even those who don't have the same views as us? Despite how unique and different we all think we are, we are more similar than we realise – we just need to look more closely. According to the National Human Genome Research Institute, humans are 99.9 per cent genetically similar – a good start, right? As we grow up, we form our values, beliefs and identities from our environment and experiences, so it stands to reason that we naturally find it easier to connect with those who have similar values, beliefs, views and experiences. But when you look deeper, you will see that we all have hopes, aspirations, stories, fears, doubts and insecurities. We all want or are working towards something more, better or different, and we are all imperfect human beings trying to find the best way possible to live with our imperfections. At times we love ourselves, hate ourselves or beat ourselves up for doing something that no-one really gives a shit about. And at times we burst with pride, happiness and hope from the simplest of things.

Through understanding more about ourselves and how we look at the world, how curious we are about the people around us and what the differences in our languages are, we can then start to see our similarities. Our differences are the things we have in common. I have created the ASK matrix (see figure 3.1) as a way of reminding ourselves what it takes to build lasting and meaningful connections in our working and personal lives.

Figure 3.1: The ASK matrix

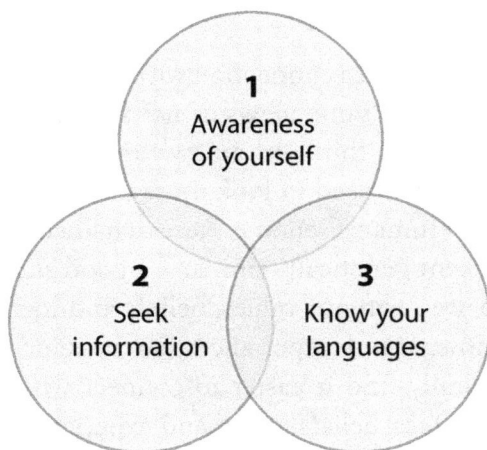

1. Awareness

We all have biases. We have to have, because our brains need ways to quickly process information – and so start to automatically put things into groups, people included. Our brains process 400 billion bits of information per second and they need to be able to sort and categorise as much as possible. So we generalise, link things together, file things away in our memories and disregard what we think is unimportant. In other words, our biases help us to navigate the world and make sense of it all. Our biases can be conscious and unconscious, negative and positive, and they affect the decisions we make on a daily basis.

But how many of us are truly aware of ourselves when we are like that? Self-awareness is a wonderful thing to have, yet it's not something we are born with, and many of us aren't particularly interested in going there. Analysing your internal biases can also be quite confronting, because we all like to think that we are genuinely nice people.

Unconscious bias

Let's look at some of the common, often unconscious, biases we have. These include:

- **Performance bias:** We tend to underestimate some people's performance and overestimate others.

- **Fundamental attribution bias:** We attribute other people's mistakes to their personality and our mistakes to the situation we find ourselves in.

- **Likeability bias:** We expect men to be assertive while we expect women to be kind and communal. So when women assert themselves more, we tend to like them less.

- **Affinity bias:** We gravitate toward people like ourselves in appearance, beliefs and background, and we tend to avoid or dislike people who are different from us. This is the reason we see 'mini-mes' everywhere in organisations.

- **Double discrimination and intersectionality:** Why stop at one! We can have bias towards people for multiple reasons – for example, race, sexual orientation, disability, gender and/or age.

- **Career recency bias:** We tend to think that the people who work for us only started work when they came to work for us. Many people, particularly mature-age workers, have had long careers and have gained much experience – which we simply don't know about because we've never asked.

You can find out what your biases are through taking an Implicit Association Test or IAT. Harvard University has a number of tests in this area on their website, and these can provide some great insights into your unconscious biases. (Go to implicit.harvard.edu to find out more, and access tests specifically created for Australians.)

Blind spots

Like biases we all have blind spots, or things that we just can't see for whatever reason. The higher we move in organisations, the less likely people are to point out we have a blind spot, which can be detrimental and dangerous for any organisation, resulting in poor decisions, favouritism and prejudice. Some common blind spots include:

- **Favouritism:** You take a liking to someone because you feel they say and do the right things, yet to others they behave differently.

- **Dislike:** On the reverse of favouritism, sometimes you can take a disliking to someone, and you just can't get past it. No matter what they do, they ain't never coming back from it.

- **Being unaware of your own behaviour:** Perhaps you're able to see when other people behave inappropriately towards others, but are unaware of the same behaviour in yourself.

- **Conspiring against others:** This is where you let your personal agenda get in the way of how you treat people.

Just being aware of your biases and blind spots isn't enough. You need to commit to taking actions that take these into consideration.

2. Seek information

We are often so busy in a world that is so demanding that we simply don't seek adequate information about the people who work for us. In his book *The 7 Habits of Highly Effective People*, Stephen Covey's fifth habit is to seek first to understand, and then to be understood. He says most of us tend to rush in with our advice or answers, without taking the time to truly understand what's being said or what the problem is. When we take the time to actually be curious, we find out far more than we often expect to. Everyone has a story, and if you stop talking and start listening you find out so much.

Seeking information helps build meaningful connections. Here are a few methods I use:

- **Active observation:** Take the time to look around you – what do you see? What are you missing? Consider this particularly in regard to the people you lead. How many people have seen an apple fall from a tree? However, it took Isaac Newton to see the force of gravity. Or think about Archimedes, who was simply taking a bath, like probably millions of people before him, yet he saw the theory of buoyancy. We all see different things in different places and seeing people is similar – until you ask what others see in them, you may not see that special thing.

- **Active listening:** One of the biggest issues that leads to miscommunication errors and missed connection is that we listen to speak, not to understand another's point of view. In a conversation, it only takes about 12 to 18 seconds of listening before your brain starts to think about what you are hearing and what you plan to say next. Our internal chatter always trumps external chatter. When we are not actively engaged in a conversation, we are actually inflicting pain on the person that we aren't listening to. The same part of the brain that experiences emotional pain experiences physical pain, so you may as well punch them in the nose. Think about that next time you ignore your children (or team members) and try to engage in active listening. You will see how useful this can be.

- **Welcoming:** Some senior leaders can come across as aloof, unapproachable or too busy, which then gives them a reputation of being out of touch with the business. When we are actively observing and listening, we are present, and this is a great way to be welcoming. Being present in a conversation says to the other person's brain that you are not a threat to them, and they will be more open to trusting you. Always ask open questions about people and get to know them, and try to ask three questions for every one statement that you make.

3. Know your languages

And, finally, the K in my ASK matrix acronym is about knowing your languages.

As a leader, you must be mindful of your words, actions and behaviours to ensure that they align, are fair and considerate, and maintain the dignity of all. This comes naturally to some, but less so to others! You must show strength with compassion and vulnerability, courage with dignity and strength, and trust while empowering your people. And, wherever possible, you must use your words, actions and behaviours to inspire your people.

What stops us from ASKing?

We are all fallible, complex human beings – and we all know this. It's no secret and we all acknowledge it. Yet, as leaders, we seem to have the perception that we have to have all the skills, all the experience and all the answers.

What stops us from admitting we don't know everything and asking for help? Fear, shame and worry. We fear we will risk our reputation if we ask someone what they would do in a similar situation. We avoid the shame of having someone suspect that we don't actually know what to do in this situation. And we worry that our reputation as a strong leader won't be upheld. When we ask someone for help, or ask what they would do, we expose ourselves to a certain level of vulnerability. We are uncomfortable because the person we ask may think that we don't know what we are doing, or that we are stupid and shouldn't really be in a position of leadership. After all, isn't that why we were put into this role? To have all the answers?

You need to break out of this fear, shame and worry, and allow yourself to be vulnerable. Using the ASK matrix allows for much greater awareness of yourself, increasing your emotional intelligence and creating connection with those you lead.

> *Vulnerability sounds like truth and feels like courage. Truth and courage aren't always comfortable, but they're never weakness.*
>
> **Brené Brown**, professor, lecturer, author and podcast host

Love in action

Southwest Airlines' mission statement is 'dedication to the highest quality of customer service delivered with a sense of warmth, friendliness, individual pride, and Company Spirit' and love is at the heart of everything they do. On 18 June 1971, they commenced their first flight from Love Field in Dallas, their flight attendants served 'Love Bites' on their planes, and ground staff issued tickets from their 'Love

Machines'. Even their New York Stock Exchange ticker symbol is LUV.

Their purpose is to 'connect People to what's important in their lives through friendly, reliable, and low-cost air travel' and they have a consistent reputation for going above and beyond to create special moments for their customers. In their induction video, they show a number of stories of employees bringing their purpose to life for their customers, and they believe they are a pivotal connection point between people and the important events in their lives. Southwest employees are 'provided the same concern, respect, and caring attitude' that they want for their customers.

Let me share some stories of employees bringing the company's purpose to life from Southwest's employee induction video. One comes from when Jessica and her family were taking her husband to the airport to start a deployment for six months to Kuwait. They were expecting to have to say goodbye at security. Kelli, a customer service representative with Southwest, asked if he was being deployed and if the family would like to go through security and say goodbye at the gate, effectively buying them an additional 30 minutes together. At the gate, when they were saying goodbye, Felix, an operations agent, asked if the children would like to say a final farewell to their father, and then arranged for them to go onto the plane, where the flight attendant paged their father and they were able to hug him one last time.

Another story from the induction video is about Tommy, who boarded an early flight without breakfast, and was one of the last few to board the plane. Following him were a mother and daughter who were unable to sit together due to the remaining available seats being located apart. Tommy offered his seat to the mother and daughter so they could sit together. When he arrived in Phoenix for a layover, he realised he couldn't get off the plane so still wasn't able to get anything to eat. He asked the flight attendant, Amy, if she happened to have any food on board that he could purchase, such as a turkey sandwich. Amy apologised but gave him a packet of chips instead. After disappearing for about 10 minutes, Amy returned with a turkey sandwich for Tommy. When he offered to pay for it, Amy replied that it was her shout because he had kindly provided his seat on the previous flight.

At the time of writing, Southwest Airlines had a valuation of US\$23 billion. According to Kristin Robertson's 2018 article, 'Southwest Airlines reveals 5 culture lessons', they also had a 4 per cent voluntary employee turnover rate, with 85 per cent of their employees feeling proud to work for them. They were the number-one organisation for the lowest number of customer complaints in the US and they had never had to lay off an employee in their 44 years of operation (prior to COVID-19).

Southwest employees are living examples of the significant benefits available when you create a culture of love in your organisation through connection, awareness and acceptance.

When you lead your people with love, you create connection, understanding and a culture of forgiveness. This enables your people to increase their discretionary effort, feel supported and safe if they fail, and increase productivity. When you are aware of your own biases and how they affect the way you see your people, you can take them into consideration and account for them. When you approach those you lead with the same forgiveness and understanding you afford your children (or you were afforded as a child), they look up to you and you inspire them. Every child wants to be like their mum and dad when they grow up, and inspiring your people is no different.

Be the leader your people want to be when they grow up – respected, admired, inspirational and, above all, loved.

Something to think about

Over the years, I have seen too many great careers shattered because of an unforgiving boss or leadership team. In each case, the employee's reputation was tarnished due to some error that was somehow unforgivable to those above. In fact, finding a story of forgiveness for this book was difficult because, even though many companies often say they have a culture of accepting mistakes and failure, leaders in these companies rarely walk this talk. However, it was not impossible.

Early in his career, a colleague of mine David was required to sign an agreement between his organisation and a vendor who would deliver works to the value of $90,000. To secure the deal, a bank guarantee was provided to David who, having never dealt with a bank guarantee before, took it in good faith. The work was only partially completed by the vendor and, after months of disagreement, negotiation and legal involvement, David's company decided to call on the bank guarantee. On review of the document, however, David discovered the guarantee had expired many months before and, therefore, was rendered worthless. David's organisation lost $90,000, due mainly to his inexperience and inability to identify the invalid document.

When he discovered his error had cost the organisation so much, David was aghast. Making such an error so early in his career seemed disastrous, and surely would cost him his job. He fronted up to his boss, fully expecting to be dismissed. What he heard was the opposite. 'David,' his boss said, 'why would I sack you when I've just invested $90,000 in your education?'

David learnt a few valuable lessons that day, one of which was on true leadership. He went on to report directly to the CEO of a $5 billion business, adding millions to its bottom line through the work he did and the teams he led. How different David's story may have been had his early boss been less forgiving.

Ways to bring love to work

- **Let people know that you value their contribution:** Say 'Thank you', 'I appreciate the work you have done' or 'You did a great job today, thanks'. Showing appreciation is as simple as that and makes people feel valued.

- **Help people to learn:** Take the time to help people to learn from what they have done, asking them how they could do things differently next time and what they learned from the experience. This shows that you are investing in their development and you want to help them grow.

- **Celebrate your wins as a team:** When your team achieves something, big or small, show them you appreciate the work they have done. You could give them the afternoon off, take them to lunch, or do a fun activity together.

- **Get to know each person:** When you take the time to get to know a person, you often find out more than you expect. You find out the things you have in common, and the experiences you share and how these have shaped your life. This builds understanding and trust in your relationships.

- **Share your stories:** When you share your stories, good and bad, you show people that we all have things we are proud of and things that we cringe over, that we make mistakes, have successes and are human just like everyone else. This shows others we are more alike than we think we are.

- **Do a team values exercise:** This allows you to ensure your company values are truly entrenched in the team environment, and everyone is clear about what is important and how actions align with beliefs. Brené Brown, author of *Dare to Lead*, offers a team values exercise along with instructions through her website daretolead.brenebrown.com. (Click the 'Operationalizing your organization's values' link.) Here you can also download the workbook for *Dare to Lead* for free.

- **Be available:** By being available when your people need you and being present in the conversation, you show them that you care about them and want to be there for them. You can also offer to help in times of pressure or when deadlines need to be met. Working beside someone is a great way to show you're one of the team.

- **Be real:** Give your people open and honest feedback. Even if you have to show a bit of tough love at times and it may be hard for them to hear, they will know your intentions come from a good place.

Chapter 4

ENVIRONMENT – WHAT YOU CREATE

At Parkhill Primary School, where my daughter attends school, visual reminders are plastered on the walls everywhere. They remind the class of the expectations of the teacher, the classroom and the school. They show the school's values of care, respect, honesty, persistence and unity. Along with a reading corner to encourage learning through books, a visual outline reminds students of the process of writing, editing and publishing to encourage a continual loop of write, review, revise and refine. Each child also has visual representations, with their own description, revealing an acceptance of who each child is without judgement.

During lessons, the teachers ask lots of questions of the children, encouraging them to consider and come up with their own answers. Silly answers are given as much consideration as sensible ones. These silly answers often generate laughter, further commentary and a sense of openness and honesty without judgement or ridicule. It's safe for each child to say what they think about something, regardless of how far-reaching or out of the box it may seem. What may seem odd or ridiculous to an adult is clearly a way of learning and experimentating for a child.

Setting clear expectations

The expectations of the teacher in my daughter's classroom have also been clearly set and understood by each child. While they all try to meet these expectations, they at times cannot. When this occurs, the teacher is swift in identifying it, addressing it and then moving on, all within a few seconds. No fuss. No contemplation or agonising over a difficult conversation and worrying about whether the child's feelings will be hurt or offended. The transgression is simply called out and addressed, and then moved on from. The children know, understand and accept this because they are clear on what is expected and on the consequences if they don't meet those expectations. The teacher has also taken the time to get to know each child, and what motivates them, what their strengths are and what weaknesses or triggers they may have. This understanding helps the teacher to support each child to play to their strengths, as well as to display tough love when required.

This understanding has helped to develop a connection between the children and teacher, as well as between the children themselves. This is the place where lifetime friendships are formed and it is clear that the children care about each other considerably. The environment in each classroom forms a mini-ecosystem that links to the broader school through the teacher, and through the school to the community. The children come to school for no other reason than their friendships and teachers, oblivious to the broader educational system.

The children are also able to engage in open debate and constructive conflict, often between themselves, with no damage to the relationships they have. I overheard a group of children, boys and girls, vigorously debate the pros and cons of Minecraft. The conversation lasted for about five minutes, with each child saying what they thought, how they disagreed with what the others were saying, and articulating their argument very well. It was surprising to see such an animated and rigorous debate between young children. At the conclusion, they all moved on, unconcerned with any risk of damage to the relationships – which, indeed, didn't appear to have occurred.

I learned more than a few things during the time I spent at Lucy's school. Setting clear expectations for those we lead is equally important in the work environment as in the school. In 2015, Gallup research found that employees with leaders who set their expectations clearly were kept more accountable to those expectations and were also more engaged. Yet only about half of all workers surveyed clearly understood what the expectations of their role were. Providing a clear set of expectations helps employees to maintain focus on what's important to ensure the job gets done; however, we find communicating these expectations to our people difficult, often only providing a poorly written role description as guidance.

Psychological safety

Questions are really powerful in creating safety because they indicate to someone that you actually want to hear their voice.

Amy Edmondson, Harvard Business School Professor

Like the children in Lucy's class, employees want the psychological safety to be able to voice their opinions, thoughts and ideas, as well as provide input into the solutions to problems. In *Leadership in the Age of Personalization*, Glenn Llopis argues that when employees are asked what they think about a problem and are able to safely provide input into the solutions, without being judged, they feel incentivised to do more. This discretionary effort is apparent in the classroom, yet somehow between primary school and adulthood we lose this will to say and do more. No doubt after being burnt too many times by bad bosses for speaking up, we are now hesitant to do so again. As already mentioned, we can also be judged and labelled in today's society very quickly, which makes us think twice about airing our thoughts and suggesting alternative solutions.

Children's desire to come to school for their friends and relationships also mimics work. Let's face it, a lot of times you will turn up to your job, even if it's the worst job you have ever had, if the people you work with are great. While some people put great consideration into aligning their values with the organisation they work for, I think most people put the relationships they have with their colleagues and leaders ahead of this. Adam Grant, Professor at the University of Pennsylvania, has studied the linkage between workplace relationships and productivity and concludes that, 'Jobs are more satisfying when they provide opportunities to form friendships. Research shows that groups of friends outperform groups of acquaintances'. They are also more collaborative, make better choices and get more done.

Leaders, like teachers, are the conduit to the organisation for their teams and must therefore play a dual role. Their first role is representing the organisation and its values and vision, and making the link between strategy and what each person does day to day. The second role is being an active member of the team they lead. It is important to earn and provide respect, understand each team member's drivers and triggers, and connect with each person on a deeper level to ensure there is psychological safety for each person to be authentic and the team to be able to engage in open, honest dialogue and constructive conflict.

Leaders must work hard to provide the environment and encouragement for their teams, like the group of children arguing over Minecraft, to engage in robust conversations without fear of being judged and the risk of damaging relationships within the team. I have always found it interesting that we find it quite acceptable to argue with each other at home in our family, yet not with the people at work. Why are we okay offering our brutal assessment to those we love the most, but then protect those we don't love nearly as much from any form of harm we perceive may occur from an argument? When we form solid, trusting relationships with those who know us best, we are able to engage in these kinds of conversations and come out the other side unscathed. So, it stands to reason that relationships in the workplace that have a similar foundation of trust will be able to sustain the same robust and rigorous debate and argument with little or no damage. A study completed by Paul Zak for Harvard University, which consisted of case studies, field experiments and surveys involving over 1000 respondents, found that organisations with teams that have high trust have 50 per cent higher productivity, 74 per cent less stress and 76 per cent more engagement. These results show that putting conscious effort into building trusting relationships is definitely worth our while.

How, then, do we provide psychological safety for our teams, enable open and constructive debate, and set clear expectations and consequences for those we lead?

Creating a psychologically safe environment

Creating a psychologically safe environment for your team means creating a space that enables people to openly and honestly share their thoughts, views and opinions, without fear of being judged, ridiculed or excluded. This is becoming harder and harder as society evolves to become more openly judgemental of people. We feel it's our right to be able to slam people for their views and opinions if they don't agree with ours. When we are put in the position of being on the receiving end of this outrage – or even seeing other people there – we learn that it isn't safe to say anything because our reputation, career and status will be put at risk. People are now afraid to say anything for fear of outraging someone.

Yet studies completed by Barbara Fredrickson from North Carolina University show that when we create psychologically safe environments for our teams to operate in, we see increases in positive emotions, with positive results: According to Fredrickson:

> *Trust, curiosity, confidence, and inspiration broaden the mind and help us build psychological, social, and physical resources. We become more open-minded, resilient, motivated, and persistent when we feel safe. Humor increases, as does solution-finding and divergent thinking – the cognitive process underlying creativity.*

(For more in this area, see 'High-performing teams need psychological safety: Here's how to create it', by Laura Delizonna.)

You can build psychological safety through:

- Focusing on building trust by being present, listening to understand, being consistent in your words and actions, and being vulnerable through sharing your stories of successes, failures and learning. A 1999 study by Harvard Business School Professor Amy Edmondson found that interpersonal trust is a key characterisation of psychologically safe teams.

- Remaining curious to help suspend judgement of others through asking questions to understand. Stephen Covey's fifth habit, 'Seek first to understand, then to be understood', not only ensures you listen more but also, through understanding more, means you're more likely to suspend judgement.

- Empowering your people by letting go. When you step back and let your people step up into their roles and actively contribute, you are sending the message that you don't have all the answers and that's okay. There are many ways to get things done and it doesn't need to be your way. Empowering people is 50 per cent their ownership and 50 per cent you letting go. It's uncomfortable and will make you feel vulnerable, but it's necessary.

Technical safety

In 2005, a company called Workday was formed by software engineers Aneel Bhusri and Dave Duffield over lunch at a diner in California. In 2019, Workday was ranked number four on *Fortune*'s list of the 100 Best Companies to Work For. As Ed Frauenheim highlights in 'How Workday focuses on improving its workplace culture every day', of its 10,000+ employees, 95 per cent ranked Workday as 'a great place to work' on the Great Place to Work Trust Index and over 90 per cent 'felt empowered' in their responses. (See www. greatplacetowork.com for more information on this Trust Index.) Employees also believed that leaders at Workday supported employees to find 'new and better ways of doing things', regardless of whether they succeeded or failed.

This type of acceptance of employees' thoughts and ideas, regardless of the outcome, shows high levels of trust between the organisation and its employees. Of Workday's six core values, employees come in first, showing the company understands and believes in their greatest asset. Their last value is profitability, but ordering their priorities in this way seems to be working, given at the time of writing they were valued at approximately US$36 billion (see macroaxis.com). Often organisations will say their people are a priority, yet their people value falls last on their list, showing a discrepancy between words and actions.

Workday, on the other hand, are continually connected to their employees through weekly surveys each Friday, to gauge the culture. Two questions from the Great Place to Work Trust Index are sent to each employee on Friday so that each quarter leaders have a complete view of Workday's culture. They are able to see trends and pinpoint areas that are doing things well, and identify hot spots if they arise. For example, through their survey they were able to identify a group of employees who were experiencing concern about career growth. Based on this, they developed a career workshop designed to help increase the skills of the group. Over the course of the next quarter, they saw the culture rating increase by seven points, showing the initiative's success.

Creating a trusting culture through connecting with your people, supporting them through both successes and failures as well as being responsive to their needs, all works to provide a psychologically safe work environment, a productive team and a profitable organisation.

Open and constructive debate

Having a diverse array of views and opinions is important to any team because it provides a broad set of perspectives, particularly when decisions need to be made. A 2017 study completed by Forbes concluded that diverse teams make better decisions 87 per cent of the time and make decisions twice as fast with half the meetings. Engaging in conflict, though, is difficult because we aren't comfortable with it, so setting up the environment to enable your team to have these conversations is critical.

Here are some ways to help establish a safe environment for your team:

- Set the ground rules for debate from the start, such as not making arguments personal, openly assigning a devil's advocate and establishing rules of engagement. These help the team to determine the standards within which they will operate.

- Understand how the team responds to conflict. The Thomas-Kilmann conflict model is a great diagnostic tool to help the team create self-awareness around their individual approach to conflict. Through understanding comes awareness and then strategies to manage.

- Maintain focus on the issue and getting to an outcome. We often focus on what went wrong and then go down the blame path. Stay focused on the problem itself and how to change the future instead of focusing on the past.

Set clear expectations and consequences

In a 2015 survey completed by US firm Harris Poll (on behalf of Interact) of more than 1000 people leaders, over a third (37 per cent) found it difficult to provide their people with feedback on their performance. Additionally, approximately 20 per cent found it difficult to give their employees clear directions. These areas are hard, I get it, but as a people leader one of the most important jobs you can do is set clear

expectations for your people along with associated consequences. Clear and concise expectations provide you with
something to measure performance against. When you and
your team have that, talking about facts with people is much
easier than using vague data points to address poor performance. Spell it out verbally and in writing so that ambiguity
is minimised. As Gallup research from 2018 highlights,
when you create this clarity for your people, they are eight
times more likely to be engaged.

Here's how to provide this kind of clarity:

- Take the time to understand what it is that you want
  your people to achieve first, so that when you need to
  communicate it, it's clear. If you don't know yourself, you
  can't expect anyone else to know.

- Spell out priorities for them using the SMART model
  of goal setting (Specific, Measurable, Achievable,
  Relevant and Timely). This is a great model to use
  because it provides you with a framework and structure
  to base your conversation on.

- Hold your people accountable if they don't deliver.
  A Gallup poll from 2019 showed that 86 per cent of
  respondents were not inspired to improve performance
  by their performance review. If people don't expect to be
  held accountable, why would they want to do any better?
  When people expect accountability, they know they
  need to deliver.

By focusing on creating a strong environment for your
people to work in, you will see improvements in creativity,
performance and accountability. Through you providing a

psychologically safe environment, people will feel comfortable to speak up and say what they think without fear of being judged, ridiculed or criticised. And when you provide this type of environment, you are also working towards a more inclusive culture for your people.

Performance also increases because your people are provided with clear feedback based on actual examples, which in turn provides tangible actions to base their development plans on. When they have a clear accountability plan based on the SMART model of goal setting, they are more likely to stick to it. If, however, they don't stick to these goals, you have clear data points with which to effectively manage performance.

Finally, your people will become more accountable for their actions. When they are more accountable, they step up and into their roles all by themselves. This in turn frees you up to focus on the work that matters, instead of wasting valuable time managing the work on behalf of your team. Holding them accountable also shows your people that you are serious about managing performance. Putting time into this up-front will set you and your team up in an environment for success.

Something to think about

At 12.10 a.m. on New Year's Eve (okay, technically New Year's Day), the first person to message me was my daughter, with four emojis, a few GIFs and a message to wish me a Happy New Year. She's 10 and my first thought was, *Why is she up so late?* Granted, it was a special night and school holidays, but since my husband and I divorced, our children have become specialists in the art of play-offs – one parent against the other – which often results in huge wins for them at the expense of breaking a consistent set of expectations and guidelines set by their parents. We work hard at trying to set our expectations and consequences for our kids and, when the system breaks, the lines blur and the wrong messages are sent.

The same applies in the work environment, where the organisation sets policies and announces initiatives fully expecting leaders to support and deliver them with their people. I have seen many leaders in organisations that espouse flexible working environments – such as working from home, part-time hours and flexi desking. However, these same leaders then complain about the unavailability of a part-time employee, try to decline requests for regular working-from-home days and issue department-wide decrees that are directly counter to the organisation-wide policy.

When we are not consistent in delivering our organisation-wide policy and guidelines, we send the message to our people that they are irrelevant and we blur the lines of expectations. This can lead to an environment that breeds deception, double standards, low trust and hypocrisy, diminishing the credibility of leaders and the system within which we operate. Remaining aligned with expectations and consequences sends a strong message of stability, clarity and reliability, reducing confusion, uncertainty and any opportunity for play-offs to arise.

Ways to create a great environment

- **Get clear:** Set your expectations and consequences with each of your people in a clear and concise way. The clearer you are, the better, because it leaves no room for the excuse of 'I didn't understand'. Clarity helps everyone to know what's expected and what will happen if it's not achieved.

- **Build trust:** Consistently building and maintaining trust with your people is an ongoing process. When you have a solid foundation of trust in a team, they are able to speak openly and freely, feel more supported and know you have their back if things go wrong.

- **Let go:** Work on letting go of the control you think you need over the outcome. Work can be achieved in many ways and have many different outcomes, and they don't all need to be the way you would do it. When you let go, your people feel more empowered and in control of the work they are doing.

- **Discuss and debate:** Encourage your team to have open conversations and voice their opinions without fear of judgement, recourse or offence. Set up the ground rules first so everyone understands and be very conscious of living by them. If you need to or you have a hairy topic, ask an external experienced facilitator to help.

- **Observe what's going on:** Listen and observe when your team comes together. This gives you great insight into the team dynamics, how they engage with each other, and if anything needs to change.

- **Be curious:** Asking more questions than providing answers is a great way to learn more about what's going on, diagnose the underlying issues and gain greater context. You could also ask, 'What would you do?' of different team members as a way to get buy in and empower your people.

- **Take risks:** Show your people that you can assess and take calculated risks. If they pay off, celebrate the win. If they don't, discuss what you learned from it. This shows that you are fallible, like everyone else in the world.

- **Volunteer for something you've never done before:** Afterwards, share with your team what you did, how you felt and what you learned. This is a great way to show people that you're okay with facing into the unknown and you have the resources to tackle it.

- **Give the benefit of the doubt:** Too often, we are quick to judge people's actions. If you give the benefit of the doubt to someone, you will show them your fairness, understanding and empathy. These are all great qualities of leaders.

Chapter 5

HEALTH – WHAT YOU SUPPORT

I want to share with you now an example closer to home. Like Gerald in chapter 3, my son, Harry, struggled at school. After he was expelled from his third school at the age of 11, we were lost as to what to do next. The most recent school he had attended was specifically for boys with behavioural issues, and if he wasn't welcome there, who else was going to take him? During this time, I spoke to the head of a school that took many children with diagnosed health issues such as Asperger's, ADHD and autism. Even though Harry had none of these diagnoses, the head seemed positive the school might be able to help, and we were hopeful. A few days later, however, she rang me to say that, after speaking with Harry's previous headmaster, she didn't think that he would be a good fit for the school. As I walked along a city street in the middle of Melbourne, my heart was breaking from the thought that no-one wanted to try to work with our son.

What seemed like our final hope was a school that we thought wasn't really going to be able to help at all. We didn't think the Frank Dando Sports Academy (FDSA) would work for Harry because he was scrawny, all arms and legs and far from sporty. What we found was a school that would offer Harry a new option for a school life, a new level of confidence and an understanding of how his health and fitness could be a strong and positive influence on his mindset.

When we first met Zac, the assistant principal, we were surprised by the school's modest environment. Situated in a large building adjacent to the home of the principal and founder, Frank Dando, it was nothing like any other stock-standard school. We have since learned there is nothing standard about FDSA. The school was established in 1980 for boys who, while intelligent, were not succeeding in mainstream schools. Their ethos, 'success in physical and outdoor education coupled with intensive teaching of core academic subjects results in success in both spheres', has been nothing short of life-changing for both Harry and our family.

An active approach

Each day starts with judo, where the boys work toward their individual capability based on belt colour. Exercise first up in the day helps the boys to eliminate any aggression or anxiety that may have occurred before school. Academic subjects of mathematics, reading and written expression are then delivered in three levels, with the boys allocated at the most appropriate level regardless of age. The physical and outdoor education also consists of daily swimming lessons and a weekly lap day, where they are required to work towards and hopefully reach a minimum of 50 laps within an hour time limit. Throughout the year, the boys participate in many outdoor activities, such as rock climbing, surf life-saving, skin diving and skiing. These are all designed to increase in level of risk and capability as the year progresses, which helps the boys to develop their skills, confidence and resilience in a safe, secure and supportive environment.

No junk food is allowed at the school and boys are encouraged to bring healthy food to graze on throughout the day. The teachers themselves role model the academic and physical education by participating in and practising the healthy lifestyle they expect of their students. They believe that the boys looking and feeling healthy has a direct influence on their self-esteem, confidence and mindset.

During his time with FDSA, we have seen Harry's confidence in his ability increase considerably and the boy who started there is very different from the young man who attends now. His body and mind are working together to increase his resilience, confidence and capability, and his attitude towards schoolwork, family and life has changed significantly for the better.

As a leader, it is very important that you and those you lead develop the capability to perform at the required level, the confidence to be able to meet and exceed expectations at work and in life, and the tools and techniques required to build and maintain resilience. Treating your own health and wellbeing with respect is as important as supporting and taking an interest in the health of those you lead, as you would with your own children. As at FDSA, a healthy culture has flow-on impacts that go beyond mind and body. By taking an active interest in diet, exercise and mindset, you will also increase the productivity and discretionary effort of both yourself and those you lead.

Diet

One of the most successful approaches we have had regarding Harry's behaviour over the years was to focus on his diet. When we removed things such as artificial colouring and flavours, fruit and vegetables high in salicylates (these include tomatoes, pineapple and strawberries) and increased food free of additives and flavour enhancers, we saw a significant reduction in his poor behaviour and a calmer, less anxious child. Recent research has also determined that a diet high in fruit, vegetables, seeds, legumes, nuts and olive oil (known as the Mediterranean diet) has a significant positive influence on depression, anxiety and stress, and can increase our productivity, creativity and overall positivity. (For more information in this area, see Ron Friedman's 2014 *Harvard Business Review* article, Audrey McGibbon and Karen Gillespie's 'Not another diet fad' from 2018 and Ashley Stahl's 2017 *Forbes* article). Your diet is one of the easiest things you can influence, requiring zero physical effort, and being completely within your control.

Exercise

According to the Australian Institute of Health and Welfare report on Australia's health released in 2018, nearly two-thirds of us (63 per cent) are overweight and 56 per cent of all adults are not physically active. By increasing each person's exercise to 30 minutes, five times per week, Australia could reduce its burden of disease by 26 per cent or approximately $4.056 billion. As with the results seen at Harry's school, Ron Freidman highlights that incorporating exercise into your daily routine has been proven to increase your mental abilities of focus, improve learning and stamina, and reduce stress. And according to J. Coulson, J. McKenna and M. Field's 'Exercising at work and self-reported work performance', exercise also helps to improve the relationships you have though improving your mood and tolerance of others. When we feel better about ourselves, we feel better about others. Couldn't we use more tolerance in the world?

Mindset

As I mentioned, Zac is the vice principal of Harry's school, and his personal philosophy is to look within to find the light – that is, you have all the answers within yourself, you are the only one who can control yourself and you don't need anything else bigger or outside of yourself to survive. His encouragement of the boys to face their fears, knowing they have the resources and mindset to handle what they are faced with, is instrumental in developing their confidence and resilience. Having a positive mindset helps us to manage our anxiety and fear at an appropriate level. This doesn't mean disregarding it, but instead means understanding that fear is a normal emotion to experience. When you develop the internal tools to be able to identify and manage fear, you are more empowered to push through it. When you feel more empowered, you are better able to face things like change and manage risks.

It is important to set the tone and support your team with health and wellbeing. As parents, our children are a reflection of ourselves. So too are those you lead. When you show your people how you live your life, they often take on the same principles. Having the self-awareness to understand how your attitudes and behaviour influence those around you is an attribute of emotional intelligence (EQ) and a critical skill required by every leader, parent and teacher. Yet EQ appears to be absent in many organisations.

In 2018 to 2019, the Institute of Managers and Leaders (IML) conducted a survey of employers to understand their needs and how universities could develop appropriate learning in order to meet those needs in their students. The research, published in 2019's *Leading Well* by David Pich and Ann Messenger, was extensive and included surveys, interviews and discussion groups involving 780 respondents. Their research was looking specifically for the competencies required by organisations, the skills that students lacked and what was required to help students to be more attractive to employers. They found that while skills such as decision-making, problem-solving and time management were strong in employees, they lacked strength in skills in the area of fostering emotional intelligence and resilience. The survey also looked at universities from the student perspective and determined that universities were 'somewhat', 'rarely' or 'not at all' helping students to develop emotional intelligence and resilience skills, and that employers felt strongly these skills should be included in tertiary level education.

I think learning EQ skills needs to start even earlier – in our homes, primary schools and high schools. Not every child goes to university, so if we leave EQ skills to higher education, we miss a great proportion of children. Also, EQ isn't solely for the domain of the business world, because leaders and employees exist everywhere. I believe teaching EQ to our children is the combined responsibility of parents, teachers and the community, and we need to start this education earlier and reinforce the learnings from multiple segments of society. If we don't teach this to our children, we will see a growing lack of empathy, increased blame, emotional outbursts, misunderstanding and an intolerance of others. Well, that sounds familiar.

> *For leaders, the first task in management has nothing to do with leading others; step one poses the challenge of knowing and managing oneself.*
> **Daniel Goleman**, psychologist and author

Health works

Fortune has listed Johnson & Johnson (J&J) as one of its most admired companies for 18 consecutive years and as number one in the pharmaceutical category for the last seven. A strong and long-established company, J&J has been operating for the last 130 years to 'keep people well at every age and every stage of life'. When they set the goal of having the healthiest workforce by 2020, they really set about walking their talk. Their view is that healthy employees bring their best self to work and this flows on to their customers.

Their three primary initiatives in the Healthy 2020 Workforce are Healthy Eating, Healthy Movement and Healthy Mind, and these are delivered to employees through their Energy for Performance® training program. The program was developed by their in-house Human Performance Institute® and covers the topics of spirituality/purpose, and mental, emotional and physical ways to direct their energy. The company also provides its employees with walking trails, standing desks and fitness centres at their facilities, all supported with a digital health tool and funding program.

J&J's goal to have a healthy workforce goes back further than this, however. In 1979, J&J introduced their Live for Life® program, designed to be a long-term, large-scale initiative to improve the health of their employees, save organisational costs associated with benefit expenses and improve overall productivity. In 2000, J&J then began to measure the impacts of their health programs across the organisation in a long-term assessment study. What they found was amazing. Overall, they found reductions in the risks associated with smoking, high cholesterol, high blood pressure and drink driving. They also found improvements in employees who weren't part of the program but were influenced by their colleagues.

(For more information on the company, see 'We set a goal to have the world's healthiest workforce by 2020' from 2018, 'The long-term impact of Johnson & Johnson's Health & Wellness Program on employee health risks' from 2002 and the J&J website – jnj.com/our-heritage.)

Start with yourself

To develop a culture of health, wellbeing and resilience for your people, you need to firstly start with yourself and your own EQ. Through reflecting on your own behaviour and how you show up, how you behave in different circumstances such as under high stress or pressure and how these impact on those around you, you can start to understand what you do and what changes you may need to make. Take some time at the end of each day to sit and reflect on the things that went well, the things that didn't go as well as you'd hoped, and what your words, actions and behaviours were in each situation. Did they help you or hinder you? How did they impact on the situation and the other parties? How could you have done things differently? When you understand the impact you have on others, you create meaning, and from meaning comes learning. Through creating time in your day for self-reflection, you are increasing your EQ and committing yourself to a mindset of curiosity, learning and ongoing development, as well as setting a positive example for your people.

It's also time to make an investment in your health and wellbeing for the benefit of both yourself and those you love. I know it's easier said than done and we are always too busy and exercise gets deprioritised when there is a deadline or critical piece of work to do. Finding time in your day to exercise can be easier, however, if you try to incorporate it into your everyday routine. As Emma Seppälä and Kim Cameron highlight in 'Proof that positive work cultures are more productive', a study of 200 employees who incorporated exercise into their day found that these employees managed their time better, were more productive and had better relationships with their colleagues. So try to incorporate activities such as team walking meetings, walking with a work friend at lunch time, parking further away or getting off public transport one or two stops earlier, or taking the stairs instead of the lift. All these are simple things that can be easily incorporated into your day.

Encouraging a healthy diet at work is also a great way to support the health and wellbeing of your people. While I understand imposing a mandatory requirement of no junk food may be taking it a stretch too far and moving into impinging on the lives of employees, encouraging a healthy diet can be just as beneficial. An organisation I worked with encouraged team lunches where everyone bought in a healthy plate and the team sat together and shared lunch. This was also a great opportunity for the team to take time away from their desks for a specific allocated lunch period instead of working through lunch. They found that through the conversation over lunch, the team members got to know each other more. This helped them to understand each other's perspectives, which had a flow-on impact in their working relationships.

Ensuring your people have a healthy balance between work and home is also a way to generate a healthy culture. I recall early in my career working in a team where it was considered humorous to have a joke about someone 'only working half the day' when they chose to leave at 4 p.m. While the joke may have had its time, the perception of someone not doing a full day's work if they leave before 5 p.m. still remains in many workplaces throughout Australia, and not just in the corporate sector. While your organisation may well espouse providing work–life balance as a drawcard to potential employees, if you don't lead by example, you run the risk of increasing burnout, stress and turnover as a result, and your employees may doubt you walk the talk in anything you say. Go home early at least once per week and encourage your people to do the same. Better still, leave early and walk home!

When you support your people to create a culture of health and wellbeing, you will find the pay-off includes increased productivity, creativity and discretionary effort and a reduction in stress, sick leave and turnover. In a Karolinska Institute study of more than 3000 employees, a positive link was found 'between leadership behavior and heart disease in employees. Stress-producing bosses are literally bad for the heart'. Additionally, a Gallup survey found that disengaged employees had '37% higher absenteeism, 49% more accidents, and 60% more errors and defects'. And further research shows that stress created in the workplace can increase voluntary employee turnover by almost 50 per cent. (All quotes and statistics from Emma Seppälä and Kim Cameron's article.)

Counter to this research, employees who exercise regularly during the week gain many benefits. According to Barry Chignell in 'Four ways exercise benefits you at work', studies have found that these employees increase their 'ability to plan, remember, simulate scenarios and make decisions' and see a positive impact on their 'alertness, energy, anger and stress levels', adding approximately $2500 worth of productivity to their employer's bottom line. Chignell also highlights that a study completed by the University of California found a positive link between corporate wellness programs and a reduction in absenteeism and improvement in productivity. Happy, energised people, doing productive work, increasing your bottom line – sounds good to me!

Wellbeing also has a positive influence on creativity, with research from 2013 highlighted by the *HuffPost* article 'Regular exercise could boost creativity' finding that employees who increased their exercise to four times per week were more creative than their more sedentary counterparts. Further, Marily Oppezzo and Daniel Schwartz in their 2014 study for Stanford University found that 'walking opens up the free flow of ideas, and it is a simple and robust solution to the goals of increasing creativity'. Personally, I can vouch for this one. If I find I'm stuck or can't think clearly, particularly when writing, I go for a walk outside. It doesn't take long for things to clarify and crystallise and when I return to my laptop, my thoughts flow.

As with Harry's school, creating a supportive culture of health and wellbeing for your people has a broad positive influence, both individually and collectively for your organisation. As your team becomes healthier, happier and more confident, you will see their resilience grow and their ability to step into and up will increase as they take on more, proactively manage risks and face their fears in a more positive and pre-emptive way.

Your role as a leader is to help your team see they have all the resources they need, right there inside them, supported by a leader who has their best interests at heart.

Something to think about

Thinking back to my childhood, I realised I have a considerable number of memories of being worried about something.
I worried about the girlfriends I had, things that were said in the playground, my grades, my teachers, my brothers, my mother. Nothing was off limits where my worry was concerned. It was like my invisible friend, there to wrap me in a comfortable blanket of safety. When I worried, I didn't have to do anything risky or scary, and the things I worried about rarely ever happened. This reinforced my worry: I told myself that if I worried about it, it wouldn't happen, so worry is good.

As I grew up, I became aware of the worry and anxiety that was around me. Two of the most influential women in my life, my mother and grandmother, were highly skilled worriers. I've no doubt this is where I developed the habit of worry, along with many of my limiting beliefs.

As parents, we teach our children our good and bad habits. Through watching and observing as a child, I learned that worry was a normal part of life, and I thought that everyone must experience this. It wasn't until I was much older that I understood what was going on and became more aware of my worry. As a parent, I am conscious of helping my children to be able to identify that worry, like all emotions, is appropriate at certain times but shouldn't become part of every day. The same applies to leadership.

Supporting your people's mental health through awareness, education and creating good habits is just as much a responsibility of leaders as it is of parents. Teach your people that being overly cautious and risk-averse is detrimental to creativity and innovation. So too, if you shy away from difficult conversations, that teaches your people to be fearful of conflict – when conflict is a normal part of life. As a leader, you must develop the self-awareness and understanding to create healthy workplaces for your people, or risk creating a culture full of bad habits.

Ways to support health at work

- **Lead by example:** When you lead a healthy lifestyle and talk about health to others, you build credibility. Walk your talk.

- **Send people home:** Agree on a day or two a week when everyone leaves at 5 p.m. (or earlier if you can manage it). Make sure you all leave together so no-one gets left behind.

- **Start late:** Come in late once or twice a week after you have dropped the kids off at school or gone to the gym before work. This shows you work to live, not live to work.

- **Get outside:** Weather permitting, have a team meeting in a park or a walking meeting. Or take a colleague or two and have lunch outside in the fresh air. It helps wake you up and gives you a dose of vitamin D.

- **Take the stairs:** An oldie but a goody! Taking the stairs instead of the lift gets the blood pumping and heart rate up, and adds to the time in your day when you're active.

- **Stand up:** Standing desks are a great way to avoid sitting for long hours. According to a study completed in 2011 at the University of Queensland (highlighted by Alice Wasley in 'Should we all have a standing desk?'), for every hour you sit you reduce your life expectancy by 22 minutes.

- **Drink more:** Water, that is! According to Nutrition Australia we should all be drinking between 2.1 and 2.6 litres (or 8 to 10 cups) of water per day. They recommend carrying a water bottle with you, drinking a glass of water with meals and snacks, and keeping fluid cool.

- **Stretch more:** Our bodies have evolved to be moved, so when we sit in one place all the time we can become stiff and sore. SafeWork recommends slow and sustained stretches, holding each for 10 to 20 seconds.

- **Host a team lunch:** Everyone can bring a plate of something healthy. This also gives everyone the opportunity to sit and have lunch, away from their work desk, and is a great way to get to know each other more.

- **Provide in-house activities:** If you have the space and budget, consider bringing in a yoga or meditation expert at lunch time. This is a great way to learn to relax, clear your mind and rejuvenate during the day.

Chapter 6

LANGUAGE – WHAT YOU SHOW

As a child, I had a loving mother, father and two older brothers. I have a couple of great memories with my family and, in particular, with my dad, whom I idolised, as most young girls do. Being the third child, and the only girl, I expect this made me milder in temperament than two rambunctious boys, so I was a bit of a relief to my parents. Indeed, my mum always told me I was a 'good' girl. My life was calm, orderly and happy – until the age of seven, when my world was torn apart by the death of my father from cancer. He was 36 years old. I recall the day he died vividly, as if it were yesterday, yet I have no memories immediately following, which I can only conclude is due to it being such a traumatic experience for me and my family.

In the years after his death, my mother married a man who was a business owner, a respected member of the community, and father of seven children. His wife had passed away also from cancer and he met my mother at a social club. He was a lovely, kind, considerate man until the day they married – at which point he turned into an alcohol-fuelled monster and my mother into a victim of domestic violence. My memories of this time include crying myself to sleep to the sound of my mother screaming and sobbing. She tried to leave him several times. On the final attempt, we had moved out into another home where, one Saturday afternoon, he presented himself at our house with a gun and threatened to kill her. Thankfully, the situation was calmed by the level-headedness of my mother and he gave up after that, never returning.

My mother's final marriage was to another businessman, who didn't beat her or yell at her and rarely drank. Again, he was kind and considerate until after they were married – at which point he convinced my mother to remove my two brothers from her care, and place them in a rental property at the ages of 17 and 15 so they were out of the way. My mother and I remained with him and, while he didn't physically beat her, his narcissism, self-absorption and inconsiderate behaviour towards others hurt her deeply. Again, I have sad memories of standing in the backyard, bare feet, surrounded by farm animals, sobbing because I was being yelled at, called stupid, told I wouldn't amount to much, and that I was brainless for not doing any one of my daily chores following his precise instructions. Looking back on my childhood, I did an awful lot of crying and had a level of anger and hurt that was seemingly undetected by others but palpable to me, sitting under the surface, carefully controlled. My most valuable life lesson here was how to manage grumpy old men! The day I turned 18, I moved out of home with my car, my minimal worldly possessions and many similar lessons.

A life full of learning about language

Learning from the experience and language of my own upbringing has been a journey in itself. I have learned much about maintaining the respect and dignity of both myself and others, that we are stronger than we think and have many resources inside us already. These resources are often available for our use when needed, yet we seldom realise it until we are faced with a situation that requires us to call upon them. I've also learned that we have a responsibility to our children to always try to lead by example, show strength, take calculated risks, and be resourceful, vulnerable, trusting and trustworthy.

If our parents are our first leaders in life, most of my role models were less than ideal. The words, actions and behaviour (or what I call 'the languages') of my two stepfathers showed a lack of the substance, character and moral fibre that all children should be entitled to see in their parents, and that all employees should see from their leaders. To think that the kind of treatment of another adult or child they displayed is in any way acceptable is beyond comprehension. Yet, sadly, this behaviour and abuse remains alive and well in homes, businesses and corporates everywhere. And somehow it is still allowed to happen, often covered up, silent and surreptitious.

In my book *The Languages of Leadership*, I talk about the six languages all leaders need to master to be more effective and influential towards their boss, their peers and those they lead. These languages relate to courage, strength, engineering, abdication, trust and vulnerability, and each one has their advantages and disadvantages when used too much or too little.

Courage

Courage is knowing that being scared witless of something isn't a reason not to do it, and understanding that fear has a role to play in the risks you take. Courage is also knowing you have the resources you need to be able to manage your fear, while continuing to move forward and find solutions along the way. If you fail, you know you will survive and learn something valuable from the process.

When you show too much courage, you can be perceived as being a bit of a cowboy and as taking too many risks, which can potentially lead to a culture of arrogance, ego and greed. Yet not being courageous enough can reduce your ability to get anything done or take risks at all, and may reduce innovation and creativity in your business.

Strength

With strength, you are able to make the tough calls when you need to, you can call out something important or that is unsaid (knowing it may make people uncomfortable), and can stand up or fight for what you believe in. You can use your strength to push your people to stretch and deliver, always with respect, fairness and dignity.

When you are too strong, you can be perceived as a hard-arse, a bully and someone no-one wants to work for or with. You will build a reputation of being difficult and increase resentment and dislike. When you aren't strong enough, however, you are perceived as weak, uninspiring and a pushover.

Engineering

Engineering is the ability to move things around in your environment to get the best out of people, relationships and situations. This helps your people to step up and shine. You can see how the system around you works, and know how to get the most out of it for the benefit of the individual, community or organisation.

When you over-engineer things, you can be perceived as manipulative, political and self-serving, in it only for yourself and whatever makes you look good. You will also spend a great amount of time and money on the wrong type of work, and on trying to get an outcome suited to your purpose. When you don't engineer situations adequately for your people to shine, you can be perceived as uninterested in their careers or development, and run the risk of losing their respect, interest and engagement.

Abdicate

When you abdicate, you are able to take a step back and out of things to give others a sense of ownership, empowering them in their work. I don't mean you sit back while others do the work: instead, you play your part and often let others take the credit for the collective results of your efforts.

When you over-abdicate, you can be perceived as lazy, indifferent and stalling the careers of others because you are taking up a position that could be used for others to achieve something in. You can appear unmotivated, selfish and unwilling to do any work. On the reverse, if you don't let others do the work, you can become a control freak – which leads to cultures of low trust, fear and accountability, and increases stress and blame.

Trust

When you use trust wisely, you are trusted by those who rely on you and you trust those you need to. You understand that trust is an ongoing process, not an event, and that you should never take advantage of it. You understand what needs to occur to build trust, and how fragile it can be. You understand that trust is at the heart of all your worthwhile relationships.

As with abdication, if you don't trust people, you increase your need for control and so create disempowered, unhappy and uncertain people. This affects your bottom line through higher staff turnover, lower profits and increased expenses. On the reverse, being overly trusting comes at a cost. Putting your trust in people who have not earned it may result in disappointment, and potential loss of profit and income. It also reduces the value of trust.

Vulnerable

Being vulnerable means you see vulnerability as a strength and understand its powerful effect on everyone around you. You are able to say if you're unsure or don't know something, which, even though this makes you feel uncomfortable, tells you when you're learning. You understand the business world is a tough environment with deeply entrenched challenges that make it hard to be vulnerable, yet you draw on your strength and courage regardless.

When you are too vulnerable, you may be perceived as weak, scared of taking risks and not knowing what you are doing. You not being vulnerable enough, however, may lead to you being perceived as cold, heartless and uncaring about those around you.

Languages in action

Jacinda Ardern was elected the Prime Minister of New Zealand on 26 October 2017 at the age of 37. At the time, she was the world's youngest female head of government and, a year later, she became the world's second head of government to give birth while in office. Since her election, she has achieved a significant and impressive list of achievements – including planting 140 million trees, extending paid parental leave and creating 92,000 jobs. Her leadership during the coronavirus pandemic has been highly praised by other world leaders, as has her leadership throughout the New Zealand terrorist attacks that killed 51 people while they prayed in mosques was one of the defining moments in her career.

Her strength during the aftermath of the attack showed through when she addressed the terrorist directly, telling him, 'You may have chosen us – we utterly reject and condemn you'. She also had the courage to call out the responsibility social media needed to take for spreading hate in society, and her sweeping gun reform laws are second only to the gun buy-back implemented by Australia following the Port Arthur massacre in April 1996.

She showed her vulnerability through her empathy when meeting with the victims' families in the following days, wearing a black head scarf, asking them what they needed and what she could do. Ardern also used her environment to show her commitment to bringing two worlds together by opening the first parliament after the attacks with the Arabic greeting of 'As-salaam alaikum' ('Peace be upon you').

Throughout this trying time, her actions showed her humility as a person and as a leader. She will always be remembered as a woman of substance and a true leader in a world that is becoming increasingly short of good leaders. Her words, actions and behaviours are synonymous with the languages of a true leader, and they spread further than her home of New Zealand. Even the Australian people voted her their most trusted politician!

Values in life

Most of my childhood male role models were excessively strong, using and abusing their power over others. They showed no courage to look at themselves and admit they had a problem, and seek help to deal with it. Through their actions, they reduced the trust of those in their lives and were unable to build trust in others. They were also unable to be vulnerable enough to talk to others about their problems and seek the help they needed to be able to have meaningful and healthy relationships.

I saw no evidence of a solid set of values in these men, which would have been able to guide them, help them to make the right decisions and keep them from doing the wrong things to other people. It's important to instil values in our children as they grow up to ensure they have a foundation from which to make decisions and determine right from wrong.

Similarly, as leaders, we need to ensure that we have good values that we use to guide our actions on a daily basis, and we display these to the people we lead.

By values I mean personal values, not organisational values – although the two will often align with each other. Values such as integrity, honesty and authenticity are great values by which to live your life, raise your children and lead your people. Equally important is helping them to realise, when the time is appropriate, that it's okay for their values to change based on their own individual experiences. Hanging on to the values of your parents can sometimes be limiting and even destructive to your relationships, both personally and professionally. When you are ardently inflexible with your values, you can appear rigid, unyielding and unforgiving, and this can be the downfall of many relationships between parents and children, and in the workplace between peers, colleagues and stakeholders. It can be hard to understand where your values come from and that they can sometimes change and some values can be difficult or uncomfortable to let go of.

Our values change as we grow, yet we often fail to recognise this as individuals and as organisations. As an organisation grows or evolves, their values must be reviewed for relevancy and applicability. If not, you run the risk of out-dated behaviour. Organisations such as Reddit, Buffer and Zappos all review and update their company values periodically to ensure they are relevant and reflect the current culture and feeling of the organisation. (See articles from Jeremy Cothran, 2017, Nicole Miller, 2018, and Patrick Thean, 2016, listed in the reference list at the end of this book, for more information.) So, too, personal values should be reviewed and updated as required to ensure they suit your purpose, goals and life as you change and grow.

As we do with our children, we must teach our people how to live their values. Consider, for example, how most organisations roll out values to their people as a guide to their expectations of required behaviour. Values such as 'Be bold' or 'Respect people' or perhaps 'Work together' – which belong to three major blue-chip corporations in Australia – are all quality values for any organisation to have. Yet, as highlighted by Chris Weller in 'Why it's so hard to speak up at work – and what to do about it', faced with a situation in which a person is not showing respect for people, studies show that 72 per cent of employees will fail to speak up or challenge that person.

Leaders honor their core values, but they are flexible in how they execute them.
Colin Powell, 65th US Secretary of State

Just-in-time learning

It is not enough that you have organisational values and then just expect your people to be equipped with the skills and experience to understand these values and know how to enact them. For example, if you tell your child how to drive a car, would it be fair to expect them to go onto a road and be prepared for all that you can experience when in control of a vehicle? Only when you are out on the road among the traffic, thinking, looking and reacting to all that is around you, can you be prepared to successfully drive a car. It takes practice, and so does living values. Knowing how to live them is as important as knowing what they are.

Recently, Harry was going to spend the day with one of his school friends during the holidays, and the plan was for them to catch a bus to a shopping centre and home again. It occurred to me before I dropped him off that he had rarely been on public transport and probably didn't understand the etiquette required. I explained to Harry that when he was on public transport, if there were minimal seats available, he was to stand and give his seat up for adults, particularly to pregnant women and elderly passengers. He assured me he would and went on his way, returning in the evening to say that he had looked around and plenty of seats were available for everyone.

When the occasion arises, you must take the opportunity to teach the people who work for you, as with children, the lessons they need to learn ahead of time so they are prepared and can practise. You then check in to see how they went. These are prime learning opportunities and provide people with more chances of retaining the learning through experiencing the situation. When we are in a specific situation that requires new learning, neuroscience tells us that the limbic portion of the brain, where our emotions are stored, becomes activated. As Deborah Rowland emphasises in 'Why leadership development isn't developing leaders', when emotions are engaged in any experience, we are more able to retain the memory and learn from it.

Leaders have the opportunity to train and coach employees in the languages required to lead effectively, with the aim of equipping people with the tools and experiences they need to manage any situation that comes their way in an organisation. This gives employees the confidence to be able to step into and create their own leadership style, and builds momentum within teams and across organisations. When you lead by example through your own leadership languages and values, you set the tone for your team and organisation. When you set the tone, others follow your lead, which in turn creates your culture. When you have a great culture, employees are happy and customers ultimately benefit, enabling everyone to reach their full potential.

Something to think about

Some years ago, Jo, a friend of mine, did some consulting work for a medium-sized business in the legal industry. The business was reviewing their values and had undertaken a culture survey of their people. The survey had highlighted a number of issues that the employees were concerned about in regards to the culture – in particular, that they didn't feel trusted to do the right thing by the organisation due to the number of checks and balances that needed to be performed for the simplest of transactions. The leadership group was surprised by this and felt that these checks and balances were in place to protect the organisation and had little to do with employees.

Jo was employed to complete a specific piece of work and had provided the leaders of the organisation with her standard consulting contract. This was accepted and signed, and Jo was able to commence the work. During the time she was there, she secured a second piece of unrelated work and agreed to commence this at the conclusion of the first. As the initial work wound down, Jo sent off another consulting contract to the leaders, anticipating no problems or concerns given the first contract had been accepted. Without receiving the second contract back, Jo continued to turn up to the workplace and started the new work, assuming things would sort themselves out in due course. Unbeknown to her, the legal team for the organisation were concerned the contract didn't fit the work.

On identifying that she was in the workplace without a finalised contract, the legal team asked Jo to leave the building. Jo was also chastised by a junior member of the legal team in front of other employees for working without a signed contract. In Jo's experience, contracts were simply a matter of course and she had completed many assignments in the past, for much larger organisations, without any formal contract in place and with no adverse consequences occurring. Jo felt that, through their actions, the leaders had questioned her integrity, honesty and ethics, with little to no consideration or explanation.

The leaders in this organisation didn't realise their actions were reinforcing what their employees had already told them in the culture survey. Their treatment of Jo in removing her from the workplace and chastising her in front of others showed they thought she couldn't be trusted to do the work without a formal contract (that is, the required checks and balances) in place. Additionally, the leaders provided no explanation or openness with Jo about the issue, making it appear secretive, uncertain and suspicious.

Ways to show your languages

- **Open up:** Talk to a trusted colleague about your concerns or problems and ask their advice. Opening up and sharing problems is a great way to practise courage in a safe environment. It also helps to get others' perspectives on the problems you face and how you may address them.

- **Role-play:** Brainstorm and role-play different scenarios with people you trust. When we practise the words and actions we would use in certain circumstances, we have more chance of recalling them when we are faced with the real thing.

- **Reflect:** Daily reflection on our words, actions and behaviours can lead to valuable insight and learning. It can also increase our productivity. Research conducted by Stefano et al. on call centre productivity found that those employees who reflected on their performance for 15 minutes each day performed 23 per cent better than those who didn't.

- **Get on the balcony:** In their book *Leadership on the Line: Staying alive through the dangers of leading*, Harvard University's Ron Heifetz and Marty Linsky develop the concept of the balcony and the dancefloor. When you are dancing on the dancefloor, you can see the other dancers on the floor around you. However, when you move to the balcony, you see the system on the floor, along with the different dance moves, groups and outliers. The same applies in business: you need to constantly move from the dance floor to the balcony to ensure you can adequately see the whole picture.

- **Empower your people:** When you empower people, they become more engaged and willing to do more for you. Empowerment is 50 per cent them owning it and 50 per cent you letting go. If you don't let go, they can't own it. It's uncomfortable but worth doing.

- **Ask questions:** In particular, ask questions that you don't know the answer to. In her book *Conversational Intelligence: How great leaders build trust and get extraordinary results*, Judith Glaser talks about the value of asking questions that you don't know the answer to. Consider using questions like, 'What do you think about that?', 'How would you handle this?' and 'What are your suggestions?'

- **Do what you say:** Always do what you say you will do, with no exception. If you need to change your mind, say so and explain why, so people understand.

Chapter 7

VISION –
WHAT YOU EMBRACE

Andrew worked as a storeman in a factory and was the father of two young girls, Emma and Olivia (all names changed). As the father of girls, he was acutely aware of the challenges they might face as they grew into young women, such as sexism, barriers to equal opportunity, violence against women and financial insecurity. Andrew's own childhood had given him significant insight into what it was like to be a woman, having been the only child of a single mother after his father died before he was born. His mother had endured many hardships throughout her life and these had had a significant influence on Andrew.

So Andrew had a vision for his girls: that by the time they were young adults, they would be financially secure enough to not be dependent on anyone, enabling them the freedom to make their own choices and the flexibility to do what made them happy. Based on the saying 'Give a man a fish and you feed him for a day. Teach a man to fish and you feed him for life', Andrew set about teaching his daughters the skills they would need to realise that vision.

Each month, Andrew would ask his daughters to help him pay the bills for the family household. They would sit together at the dining table and look at the bank statements for the family bank account. They would review income for the month, prepare the cheques for each of the bills that had arrived, tally the total and do a bank reconciliation on the account. They would address the envelopes, apply the stamps and mail them the next day. They learned the value of money, the importance of managing it well and how to run the business of living.

Each of his daughters also ran their own business from the age of 13. Emma would make chocolate chip biscuits each weekend, package them up and send them off with Andrew to the factory to sell to his colleagues. Andrew helped Emma to ensure that each biscuit met a particular size and quality standard and he would refuse to take the biscuits that did not meet the agreed standard. Andrew also helped Emma to look at the packaging and marketing of the biscuits to ensure they were appealing and priced competitively.

Olivia would collect and sell eggs from the family chickens. Each day she would collect the eggs, wash and dry them, and check each one for cracks. She would then package them up and sell them to friends and neighbours. She fed the chickens each day and ensured they were looked after, healthy and happy. Each week, the girls would sit with Andrew and tally their earnings, calculate expenses and deposit their profits into their bank accounts.

In their late teens, both girls had the deposit for their own homes and were able to purchase their properties independently. They were able to show the bank that they had a consistent and pragmatic savings routine, and so prove themselves low security risks. Now in their late twenties, both girls have investment properties as well as their own homes, thanks to the purposeful actions and strategic planning of Andrew.

Having purpose in the work you do and thinking strategically about how to achieve your goals are the two elements of creating a great vision for your family and those you lead. The two are integral in determining the aspirational goals or the vision you want to achieve.

The purpose of purpose

Underlying vision is your purpose. Having a clear purpose helps to develop your vision of where you are going and defines the meaning in the actions you will use to get there. Your purpose is like the rudder of a boat: it steers you in the direction you are going, and adjusting it and allowing it to evolve along the way is normal and natural in the journey of your life. Andrew's purpose was one of security and independence, and this drove his desire to help his daughters to become self-sufficient, independent and confident in their ability to manage their finances. His purpose guided his actions in teaching the value of money and how it is earned, and the value in producing quality outputs and how this linked to customer satisfaction and sales.

Research also supports the value of having purpose as the foundation for successful leadership. After a 2016 study completed by Emma Russell and Chris Underwood, they concluded that purpose, instead of a distinct set of leadership characteristics or a distinct leadership style, led to successful leadership. They also concluded that 'leaders with purpose define success as more than business or financial objectives – for example, leaving a legacy'.

As leaders, we don't think enough about the legacy we leave for those around us. If we did, we would see far fewer poorly behaving leaders – think Donald Trump, Kenneth Lay and Jeff Skilling (from Enron) and Martha Stewart. There is no time like the present to consider what your leadership legacy will be and make the necessary changes to ensure it's a positive or beneficial one for all you have worked with. Again, having purpose and meaning in the work you do is reflected in your approach to work and permeates throughout your team and organisation. Everyone who works with you can see it and feel it, and your legacy has a positive impact even after you've left.

Having a strategy

Sadly, you can't predict the future. If you could, you'd be sitting on a banana lounge drinking cocktails reading something other than a business book, I expect. The next best thing to predicting the future is creating a strategy, because it gives you above-average odds of achieving what you want to. At the very least, a strategy provides a plan for achieving something while mitigating the foreseeable risks. At best, you create the future that you want to and achieve more than what you set out to.

Andrew's strategy for his daughters was to help them develop the skills they needed to become financially independent in a future that was largely unknown. He developed the strategy based on his best educated assumptions about what his daughters might need in the future, whether this goal was realistically achievable and how best to use their existing strengths and resources. His daughters then went on to achieve even more than Andrew's original strategy.

Organisations go to great lengths to create strategic plans each year. However, as Panu Kause highlights in 'So (you and) your people don't understand your strategy?', a study completed in 2016 in Finland found that a mere 12 per cent of organisations were actually able to implement their strategy successfully. Approximately 70 per cent of strategic initiatives failed and less than 20 per cent of employees were able to articulate what their organisational strategy actually was. Additionally, in a Gallup *State of the American Workplace* report from 2018, only 22 per cent of their respondents agreed that their leaders had 'a clear direction' for the company. In other words, 78 per cent of respondents either didn't know their company strategy or thought their leaders didn't have one. As leaders, we may be good at developing a strategy but we clearly have work to do in helping our people understand it.

Creating a vision

To create a great vision for your people, you need to have both a strategy and a clear purpose, as shown in figure 7.1. If you don't have purpose in your life, you can float along aimlessly, with no real meaning in the work you are doing. Similarly, if you don't have a strategy or plan for where you are going, you are often spontaneous in your actions.

Figure 7.1: Strategy combined with purpose

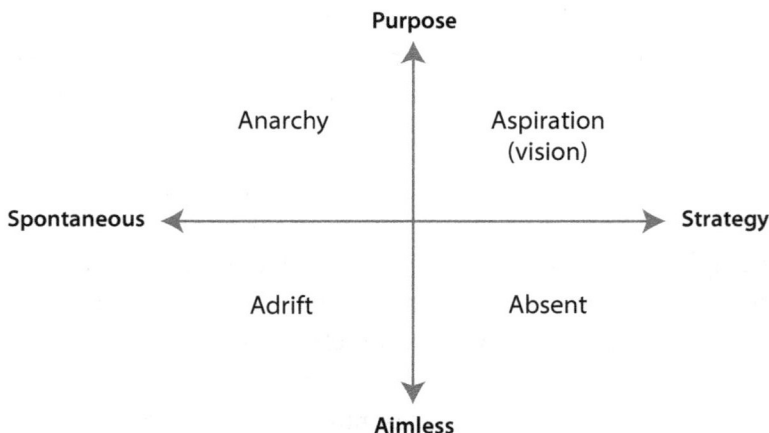

As shown in figure 7.1, four types of outcomes are influenced by having (or not having) a purpose and a strategy. These outcomes are:

1. **Adrift:** When you have no clearly defined purpose and your actions are spontaneous and reactive to your environment, you drift along through life. What you are doing and why is unclear, and achieving anything usually happens in spite of yourself or your actions.

2. **Absent:** When you have a strategy or action plan to get somewhere, yet you are aimless and without a purpose, you become transactional, completing your strategy with no link to any kind of value. Your intention and meaning are absent.

3. **Anarchy:** When you have a clear purpose but are spontaneous and reactionary instead of having actions outlined by a clear strategy, anarchy reigns. You are reactive to your environment and overly sensitive to the market. You have no clear way of staying the course when your environment becomes volatile.

4. **Aspiration (vision):** When you are clear on your purpose and understand why you are here, you're able to link the work you do every day to where you are going. Your strategy helps to define the objectives and actions along the way and you create a clear and compelling aspiration or vision for the future.

If you can clearly articulate your purpose for being as well as your strategy for achieving this purpose, the two come together intrinsically to create a compelling vision for the future.

When purpose and strategy align

Patagonia is an outdoor clothing retailer founded in 1973 by Yvon Chouinard in the US. Yvon was a keen rock climber and environmentalist and, after noticing how his tools were damaging the rock face, he started to develop his own equipment. On a climbing trip to Scotland, he also purchased a rugby jersey to climb in and noticed the durability of the material along with the way the collar protected his neck from the slings. These insights inspired the worldwide brand that Patagonia has now become.

Patagonia's mission or purpose is to 'Build the best product, cause no unnecessary harm, use business to inspire and implement solutions to the environmental crisis'. Their values include collaboration, transparency and improvement. Patagonia also spends approximately US$1 million each year on subsidised childcare for their employees because they believe that employees should be able to work while they raise their family, not the reverse. They also encourage their employees to pursue sport interests and devote time to charities and not-for-profit organisations. Throughout their supply chain, Patagonia ensures their products are created in safe and fair environments with humane and legal working conditions. Patagonia lives their purpose.

Patagonia's strategy is also unique. Their approach to anti-consumerism through their 'Don't buy this jacket' campaign in 2011 encouraged consumers to think carefully about what they consume and to buy quality products that are repairable and thoughtfully produced. They also partner with Fair Trade USA to highlight the working conditions of factory workers and give back some of their profits. Through their Worn Wear program, they sell worn and recrafted items, and help consumers repair their clothing through providing repair guides for common items. And through storytelling in videos, they create activists from their consumers by encouraging them to be a part of their environmental causes.

Patagonia is a living example of how having a clear purpose for the organisation connects employees and consumers in a way that unites behind its foundation. The strategy helps to show the way forward and what the future could look like when they achieve the outcomes they aspire to. When the two come together, they create a powerful entity supported by employees and loyal consumers who all want the same thing. For Patagonia, this also created a profitable and sustainable organisation – in 2018, Forbes estimated founder Yvon Chouinard's net worth was $1.5 billion. Proof enough.

Effort and courage are not enough without purpose and direction.

John F. Kennedy, 35th President of the United States of America

Finding your purpose

In *The Advantage*, Patrick Lencioni talks about leadership teams needing to create clarity for themselves and their organisations by answering six questions, the first of which is, 'Why do we exist?' This is about understanding the purpose of the organisation to help create an understanding of why your people actually show up for work each day. Your purpose needs to be idealistic – in the case of Patagonia, the purpose of building great products with reduced harm to the environment and inspiring solutions to the environmental crisis meets that requirement. This is a purpose that will guide the organisation through thick and thin, good times and bad.

In the work I do with leadership teams to help to define their purpose, the 'why' question is very helpful. Similar to the technique used in process improvement for finding the root cause of a process defect or problem, by asking 'Why?' multiple times, you are able to dive more deeply into the reasons and rationale for what you do. For example, a hairdressing salon may determine that they are here to cut, colour and style hair. But the real reason is deeper than this. Asking 'Why?' repeatedly draws this out:

1. We are here to cut, colour and style hair. Why?

2. To help people to look good. Why?

3. When people look good, they feel good. Why?

4. When people feel good, they are happier. Why?

5. When people are happy the world is a happier place.

This series of questions then provides the salon's real purpose: We are in the business of creating a happier world, one head at a time.

By the way, Lencioni recommends you stop one step shy of creating world peace.

Creating your strategy

Your strategy is like your roadmap to the future (or your Google Maps for those not familiar with the hard copy version). As in most long road trips, many milestones appear along the way that help you to ensure you are making progress. First, though, you need to know where you are going.

In *Corpus RIOS: The how and what of business strategy,* Christopher Tipler outlines his RIOS model – the Realistic Imagination Of Success, which defines your endpoint in your journey. Having a clear RIOS helps you to determine the conditions required for the journey and the potential risks you may encounter, and aids the development of a realistic belief in what it is possible to achieve. Essentially, if you can imagine a future and believe it's realistic, you can bring it into being.

While your strategy is your 'what', your milestones, tactics and measurements determine the 'how'. I've seen organisations develop a laundry list of actions to support their strategy – and wonder why, in 12 months' time, they have achieved only a small number of their actions. As with your strategy, so too should your objectives and actions be realistic. They should also be minimal, and I always recommend a maximum of four. If nothing else, you can dedicate one week per month to each objective, or a quarter each year.

Your strategy should also be reviewed regularly to track your progress and make amendments as required. In research published in the *Harvard Business Review* in 2005, Robert Kaplan and David Norton determined that 85 per cent of leadership teams spent less than an hour each month reviewing their strategy, and 50 per cent spent no time reviewing it. Your strategy should be treated as a living, working document, with successful companies reviewing their strategy in detail monthly, dedicating three to four hours to it.

Ditching the double speak and jargon

Giving a lot of consideration to how you communicate your purpose, strategy and vision is a critical part of the process. If fewer than 20 per cent of employees are able to articulate their organisational strategy, clearly the message isn't being communicated well or often enough. Communicating visions and strategies often also involves great terms such as 'value proposition', 'paradigm shift', 'lateral thinking' and 'core competencies'. Seriously, I find these terms frustrating and I know what they mean. If even one audience member doesn't understand the language you're using, you will lose them and they will tune out. When communicating your strategy, you want every single person to understand, so explain it like you are talking to a teenager.

In *Real Communication: How to be you and lead true*, Gabrielle Dolan talks about the value of being authentic in your communication with those you lead. Through using plain English, reducing jargon and acronyms and sharing personal stories, you show your respect for people and their time, work to build and increase trust and show you are relatable and approachable. In the same way, taking the time and effort to create a communication plan that is clear, concise and easy to understand by every member of your organisation will save you a lot of time and money down the track, particularly if 70 per cent of strategic initiatives fail.

The advantages to organisations of having a clear purpose, strategy and vision have been well researched and documented. For example, according to Gallup research from 2017, ensuring your people understand and connect with your core strategic components leads to increased profitability, reduced staff turnover and safety incidents. And as Juliette Denny highlights in 'Why your employees should know the business mission', research shows that an impressive 73 per cent of employees who work in an organisation with a clearly defined purpose report that they are engaged, in comparison with just 23 per cent in organisations without. These organisations with a clearly defined purpose also report increases to productivity, trust and retention rates.

For Andrew from the beginning of the chapter, having a clear understanding of his purpose and creating a well thought out strategy meant he was able to create a vision for his daughters using a realistic imagination of success. He has seen the benefits for his daughters and the legacy that he has created as a father and the girls' first leader in life. By taking the time to invest in these activities, he has been able to instil personal ethics, valuable learning and priceless memories within his family. It's possible to create the same experiences within your work family also, leaving a leadership legacy worth building on.

Something to think about

As the boys in my son's school progress, they are encouraged to start to think about their transition into the working world and the work they will do when they leave school. Some of the boys already have part-time jobs, which helps them to understand how work works. As the school only goes to grade 10, some of the boys will move on to mainstream schools or Technical and Further Education (TAFE) colleges to complete their final two senior years of school. Others won't complete grade 12 and will instead commence a trade certificate such as in plumbing or electrical. In all cases, the school tries to prepare the boys as much as possible for this transition.

During the final year of schooling for each boy, the lessons start to focus more on the type of practical information they will need out in the real world. For example, one of the boys has decided he will start a plumbing apprenticeship at the end of the year. This means the focus for his mathematics learning has shifted to the more practical maths used in the plumbing world, and his work involves aspects such as calculating job estimates, cost of materials and labour, and profit. He is also learning to calculate water pressure, angles, volume and velocity.

The vision for the boys is that they will go out into the world and become productive, reliable and valuable employees. The strategy employed by the school is to teach the relevant educational requirements for performing in a particular job, which will give the boys the confidence to pursue the job they want, knowing they have some of the skills already. They create a sense of purpose by understanding how the work they do will help them to secure a job and become contributing members of society. After all, isn't that what we all want for our children?

Ways to embrace your vision at work

- **Find your purpose:** Use the repeating 'Why?' technique from earlier in the chapter with your team. Remember, don't fill your responses with corporate jargon – keep it real and keep questioning. You'll know your purpose when you see it, because it will feel right.

- **Build a strategy:** Find your RIOS, your Realistic Imagination Of Success, by including your team in a brainstorming session. Always remember to set your ground rules first – such as creativity is encouraged and nothing is off the table when you look for ideas. Then determine which ones are realistic and achievable in your timeframe.

- **Find your story:** Truly understanding and capturing your story is a benefit to all organisations. Once you understand what your story is, you can always link back to it with your purpose, strategy and vision. This helps to provide your people with the valuable context that links to the 'what' you do. When people can create a link between the 'what' and the 'why', things make sense and meaning is created.

- **Be prepared to not know:** Leaders often feel that they have to have the answers to everything, but this isn't the case. Admitting that you don't know something and asking your people to contribute with their thoughts and ideas creates their buy-in. When people feel that they have contributed to the answers, they become more invested in achieving what they need to.

- **Use plain English:** When you communicate anything to your team or organisation, keep it simple. When you use too many big words, you lose people, they can't follow what you're saying and they tune out. Try explaining your vision or strategy to your grandmother first – if she gets it, you're on the right path.

- **Become a cracked record:** People need to hear things many times and in many forms before they remember something. That's why you see ads for the same product on TV, in newspapers and online. The same applies to your vision. Everything you say and do needs to be linked back to your purpose, strategy or vision, so people understand and remember it. Mixing up your channels – through using words, visuals, video and different symbols – also helps.

Chapter 8

CREATING YOUR
WORK FAMILY

In the early 1990s my mother, Shirley, was diagnosed with an oral (or mouth) cancer. This was surprising considering she had never smoked. Her initial operation was to remove the tumour on her tongue, and this was considered successful. The cancer returned a few years later, which resulted in another operation to remove her tongue completely. She lived quite successfully like this for the next five years. She was truly an amazing woman, and her achievements were impressive. I would chat to her on the phone every other night, understanding everything she said quite clearly.

She was working as an accountant at the time and decided that she wanted to find another job, so she applied for a role in the city. She went through the normal application process, interview and reference checks and her application was successful. I was in awe of a company that would employ a woman purely on her merit, thinking far less about her disability. She commenced her new role and loved it.

A month later, she went for a routine check with her doctor and they discovered a lump on the carotid artery, the main blood supply between the body and brain. When she rang me to tell me she would need to have another operation to remove the lump, I was concerned and worried. Surely she had been through more than enough in her life. I was sad and upset for her.

The next day, the day before Melbourne Cup in November 1999, she sent me an email. She said:

> *Don't worry about it because as you know worry doesn't do anything for anything. There is nothing we can do except leave it in the hands of the doctors. When I was your age, I was the same, felt the same and it is such a big worry – but as you get older, perhaps you get wiser, or perhaps it is just me and what I have been through, but you learn to accept the things that you cannot control and learn that there are other people who are better equipped at it than you are... take it easy and rest. Even have a good cry if you think it will help. Just remember also that if I die then, again there is nothing you can do. Don't get angry or hurt, you just have to accept that it was my time to go.*

After the operation the following day, my mother suffered a stroke and passed away late that evening. It was sudden and devastating to lose her at the age of 60, and the shock of losing someone so suddenly had a profound effect on my life. As I grieved for her, I recall reading her email many times and her words providing some level of comfort to me.

After 20 years, I still have a copy of her email and her phone number remains recorded in my phone.

Faced with such a difficult and uncertain time, my mother's strength, courage and vulnerability were inspirational. Her absolute faith in her surgeon stemmed from her belief and trust he would do the best possible job he could for her. She admired him and trusted in his ability to do his job. She also accepted that this was beyond her control and she couldn't influence the outcome, regardless of what it was. She could only prepare for what she could control in her environment and provide love and support to those around her to help them to be able to manage either way. Her consideration for the wellbeing of others, and to ensure that we were prepared for the future – even a future without her – are testament to the woman I admired.

She was one of the great leaders in my life.

All-the-time leadership

Sadly, we usually see great leadership in circumstances that are unfortunate, devastating or distressing. It seems that in these types of situations, like Mum, people rise to the challenge of leadership and show that they are worth following, worthy of your support and true leaders. When we see great leadership we recognise it instantly. A recent example I have already mentioned was Jacinda Ardern, Prime Minister of New Zealand, who responded with great leadership in the wake of the 2019 terror attacks and to the COVID-19 pandemic. Another example is Malala Yousafzai, who at the age of 11 was shot by the Taliban for her outspoken views on female rights to education. She has recovered and continues to work in this area. And another is Bono, lead singer of U2, who has persuaded global heads of government to write off debt for some of the world's poorest countries, along with encouraging them to increase funds for AIDS support. (For these reasons, Bono was included on *Fortune*'s 2014 list of the world's 50 greatest leaders.)

Like these leaders, we must make leadership an everyday thing – something that is ingrained into our psyche, and a natural behaviour that would be out of place if we didn't see it. We shouldn't have to wait for it. Yet, we find it very difficult to actually show leadership in this way. In research completed by Joseph Grenny and David Maxfield and outlined in their book *Crucial Conversations*, they found that when people are faced with a situation that requires them to speak up and show leadership, 72 per cent will fail to do so. In addition, they found that avoiding doing so costs an average of $7500 in lost productivity, because those who should be leading are instead discussing the issue with others, worrying about the problem or doing superfluous work. It's time we started teaching our people how to be leaders, every day, in every way.

You need to create teams and workplaces that:

- practise love through connection, inclusiveness, self-awareness and respect

- operate in an environment that is psychologically safe, have clear expectations and consequences and engage in open and constructive conflict

- encourage and support their people to live healthy and happy lives, physically and mentally
- are led by great role models who show strength, courage, trust and vulnerability as part of their daily routine
- have leaders who have purpose, a strategy and a clear way to get there.

Only then will your organisations and your people reach their true potential. To ensure you can live these five principles, you also need to consider a broader perspective, ensure you are supported to lead as effectively as you can, and continually reflect on the insight you have, what's already in plain sight and the foresight you need. These will help you to create your work family.

It's bigger than you

In organisations everywhere, no-one, ever, anywhere, does anything alone. Your dependence and interdependence with others is intrinsic to you and your team's success. If you think that you can do your job all on your own, without anyone's help, you're kidding yourself. As my mother's final email to me shows, she knew this was bigger than her and that, for her, caring for her family was more important than what she was experiencing. Your job is bigger than just you, and bringing your work family together, united and moving in the same direction, is essential to achieving your goals and vision for the future.

In 2014, psychologist Dr Fred Kiel conducted research into the impact of CEOs who displayed behaviours such as 'standing up for what's right, expressing concern for the common good, letting go of mistakes (their own and others), and showing empathy' within their organisations. Kiel's findings, published in *Return on Character*, showed that these CEOs produced an average return of 9.35 per cent, compared with CEOs who were more 'self-focused' producing returns of only 1.93 per cent on average. These behaviours from the very top will permeate throughout the organisation, having an impact on leaders, employees and customers.

As a parent, one of the things you realise early on is that it isn't about you anymore. You can no longer operate in the single or 'married couple no kids' world that you were used to. When you are a family, you have to put aside your singular self-interest for the greater good of your family's interests. You put yourself second for the good of the whole. The same applies to leaders and employees alike.

When we start to put the team or organisation ahead of our own interests, and we operate in a caring, considerate and supportive organisation, we want to do more than just our job. We want to create more than what is needed and we want to be more than we thought we could be, because we can see the future, feel the future and be part of the future, together.

Move beyond sole parenting

Raising children is hard work, and harder still if you are on your own. In the 2016 Australian Census, figures released by the Australia Bureau of Statistics (ABS) showed that

13 per cent of households were a single-parent family. In these families, the care and running of the family falls to one person, and finding support is critical. This can come in the form of grandparents, friends, extended family members or even outsourcing from time to time. So the adage 'it takes a community to raise children' still applies, and it also applies to leading people. Leading teams is a lot like single parenting. You need to make decisions on your own, look after each and every one of your team members by yourself, and take responsibility for each of them.

Securing support outside of your team to help to develop your people has proven benefits. For example, finding external mentors for some of your people helps to broaden their perspective and network, and increase organisational awareness. A study completed in 2012 for the University of Southampton on the benefits of mentoring found that mentees saw improvements such as boosted productivity and time management; enhanced wellbeing, confidence and self-esteem; and increased job retention.

Similarly, having a support network for yourself will help you to be a better leader. Internally, ensuring you are establishing good relationships with your support functions such as human resources, finance and operations will help you to understand and support your people, business and industry, and provide you with valuable knowledge, contacts and resources.

You also need to develop a strong external network. In her book *It's Who You Know: How a network of 12 key people can fast-track your success,* Janine Garner says 'a strong, connected and mutually beneficial network provides you with a series of stepping stones to success' and that having a supportive network helps to boost confidence, support your decision-making and achieve your goals. Your external network also helps you to stay across what's going on in your industry, which can help with recruitment, strategic planning and sourcing new ideas.

Be conscious of work 'families'

I think it's important to note that not everyone has what they consider to be a positive family experience. Sadly, some families experience dysfunction, separation and even violence, and this has a lasting impact. Therefore, using the term 'family' to describe your team may not be the right approach and should be considered with sensitivity for your team members. Terms such as 'tribe', used by Seth Godin in his 2009 TED Talk 'The Tribes We Lead', or 'clan' are great alternatives. Being conscious and considerate of what's suitable is key here; essentially, though, the principles remain consistent.

Building your work family

In the introduction, I spoke about the value of having insight, seeing what's in plain sight, and establishing foresight. We can use these three concepts in each of my five core leadership principles to establish your work family, because each provides a different perspective or lens to help you to build and develop your relationships and create productive and cohesive teams. By overlaying them across each of the five core areas of Love, Environment, Health, Language and Vision, you can gain a unique perspective.

Love

Here's how the three different ways of seeing can apply within the Love principle:

- **Insight:** What are your biases and blind spots and how are they affecting the way you lead your team? Do they prevent you from establishing a true connection with those you work with or lead? What insight into your people do you have? How can you get to know them so that you understand their stories, how they view things and where they operate from? This context helps to establish connection as well as providing understanding into how each team member approaches things. This all helps to create connection, understanding and forgiveness.

- **Plain sight:** What's already happening in your team? What existing relationships can you leverage? Who are you already connected with, and why? What is different about this relationship compared with others? Are you already actively including your people in decision-making by asking their point of view? If not, what is stopping you from asking? Do you already celebrate success with your team? Or say thank you for their contribution? By seeing what's in front of you to work with, you can then determine what's missing to be able to plan for the future.

- **Foresight:** What do you need to put in place for the future to be able to move to a more connected and collaborative team? What do you want your ideal team to look like? Speak like? Feel like? How can you build an inclusive team? What behaviours need to change? What do you need to do to create a culture of acceptance, inclusiveness and forgiveness? These all provide input into your strategy and vision for the future.

Environment

For Environment, think about the following:

- **Insight:** What do you already know about what your people do? Do you understand what each employee or team does, and how this impacts on other areas or functions? What upstream and downstream impacts are there when things go wrong or right? Are your people already clear about your expectations? Do your people know the consequences if they don't meet your expectations?

- **Plain sight:** Is your environment already psychologically safe for your people? How do they engage with each other right now? What team rules or norms already exist and how do they influence how your people talk to each other? How do people voice their opinions, good or bad? How does communication already happen within the team?

- **Foresight:** What do you want the environment to look like in the future? What needs to change from your plain sight views to get to where you want to be? How can you be clearer on your expectations and consequences in future? How can you use your colleagues or broader networks to help to provide a supportive environment?

Health

The Health principle can be looked at in the following ways:

- **Insight:** What do you know about each member of your team in regards to their health? What about the health and wellbeing of their family members? How do you approach your own health and wellbeing? What health and wellbeing goals do each of your people have? What are your people working towards personally?

- **Plain sight:** What do you see happening now with start and finish times? Is the current approach to health in your team positive or negative? Do you actively support your people with their health? Do you currently look after yourself and set a good example? What support already exists for the mental health of your people?

- **Foresight:** What can you do in future to support a healthy approach to life? Do you need to plan to do things differently? How can you better use your environment to support the health and wellbeing of your people? What organisational changes can you sponsor to make sustainable changes?

Language

The three ways of seeing can be applied to the Language principle as follows:

- **Insight:** How do your people see you as a leader? What feedback have you received from them? What stories have your people shared with you that give you insight into their lives? Do you know what aspirations and goals your people have? How do these align to their development plans? How do your people's personal values align to your team or organisational values?

- **Plain sight:** How do you currently reflect on your words, actions and behaviours? What is your current approach to risks? How do you support your people when they fail? How do you put your people into situations that will help them learn and grow? What things do you do already to build and maintain trust? How does your team currently behave together?

- **Foresight:** When you consider how your team currently behave together, does it align with your future plans? What needs to be in place to change or support the behaviours you want to see? How do you create a more supportive behaviour for failure? How do you develop each team member to get them to be at their best?

Vision

And Vision can include the following:

- **Insight:** Can you explain your current strategy and vision to your mother or grandmother and does she understand it? Are you able to draw a picture of your vision on a page and describe it in 50 words or fewer? Do you know what your purpose is? Do you have a Realistic Imagination of Success (RIOS)? Do your people know, and can they clearly state your current strategy and vision? Do your people know what needs to be done to achieve your vision?

- **Plain sight:** How does the work each team is currently doing link to your strategy? What happens when you ask a team member to explain your strategy? Can your employees clearly link what they do now to the strategy? Do your people know which part of your strategy is currently underway? What strategy meetings do you currently have with your leaders or team members? How do they update and track their progress?

- **Foresight:** What do you need to put in place to ensure that everyone understands how their jobs link to the delivery of your organisation's strategy and vision? What needs to change to make sure every employee understands and knows the strategy and vision and how it will be achieved? How do you plan to keep track of the deliverables to ensure your team achieves its goals?

The questions I've included for each of the core principles are certainly not exhaustive. They are there to help you to think about the insight you have or need, what's already occurring and why, and what you need to put in place going forward to give you and your team as much probability of success as possible in achieving what you set out to.

Learning to juggle

I've always struggled to remember people's names. Usually within 10 seconds of me being introduced to someone, their name has left my memory and I am always frustrated by it. To help with this I decided to complete an online course to improve my memory, and part of the training was to learn to juggle. As I started to juggle with three pairs of socks (easier, I'm told, because they don't bounce around if you drop them), I naturally dropped many of them. I would pick them back up and continue on, progressively improving my technique.

As a parent, I often feel like I'm juggling so many things at once – and I also usually feel that if I drop something, the whole world will come crashing down around me. I often do drop the balls I have in the air, however, and I've come to learn that it's okay. I pick them up again and keep going. The point of the exercise is to keep going, keep trying, and keep picking them up.

The same principle applies with leading teams. I can guarantee at times that you will drop at least one of the balls you have in the air, and that's okay too. But if you keep going, keep trying and keep picking them up, like me you will eventually find your rhythm and technique.

As with parenting, leadership is equal parts hard work, persistence and determination, and the rewards are momentous and incredibly satisfying.

If you stick with it, before you know it, you'll be leading a team that is connected, performing and inspired by your leadership. You'll be leading a family you're proud to be part of.

> *Leadership is not about titles, positions, or flow charts. It is about one life influencing another.*
> **John Maxwell**, author and speaker

FINAL WORDS

Two of the hardest things I have done in my life are raising children and leading people. Yet they remain the most rewarding. When I look at my children today, I often think about how far they have already come in such a short amount of time, and how much further they have to go. As a parent, the most you can hope for is that you do a good enough job that your children live happy and fulfilled lives. This also applies to leadership, and your responsibility to your people is the same – that the time they spend with you at work is happy, fulfilling and purposeful. As with parenting, you have a big role to play in that.

It's a responsibility worth your investment to help your people to be the best that they can be – through creating a work team that is supportive and connected; creating a safe, healthy and happy environment in which they can be themselves; and through being a leader who walks their talk and ensures that everyone is clear on the way forward and how to get there.

If you take only one thing from this book, let it be that you already have the experience needed to be a great leader – either from raising your own children or by learning from your parents. Like most people, I have had good and bad experiences from both. In my life, pretty much everything is far from perfect. That's normal. What you can do, though, is learn from each and every experience and put in place strategies to manage them. Never be afraid to try out different ways of doing things until you find one that works.

Be courageous, be strong and keep going.

Wendy

> *Success isn't about how much money you make; it's about the difference you make in people's lives.*
> **Michelle Obama**

KEEP IN TOUCH

Thanks so much for reading my book. I hope you enjoyed it as much as I enjoyed writing it. I also hope that it has given you something useful that you can easily apply to your workplace. The most rewarding part of the job I do is hearing about my clients' successes, particularly when I have helped in some way.

If you or your organisation would like help with becoming a better leader or more effective leadership team, I would love the opportunity to work with you. I can tailor a coaching program or leadership development package to suit your needs. I can also speak at your function or event, so please contact me for more information.

You can find out more about me on my website wendyborn. com.au or you can contact me directly at wendy@wendyborn. com.au.

I wish you all the very best in putting your work family together and inspiring those around you as you do.

Wendy

REFERENCES AND FURTHER READING

Introduction

Funkhouser, A. & Schredl, M. (2014) 'Deja vecu and deja visite similarities and differences: Initial results from an online investigation', *Journal of Consciousness Studies*

Maccoby, M. (2004) 'Why people follow the leader: The power of transference', *Harvard Business Review*

'Transference' (2019) *Good Therapy* blog, https://www.goodtherapy.org/blog/psychpedia/transference

Chapter 1

Adonis, J. (2017) 'Cyberbullying: Adults are worse than children', *The Sydney Morning Herald*

Australian Institute of Health and Welfare (2018) 'Australia's health 2018: In brief'. Cat. no. AUS 222. Canberra: AIHW

Colino, S. (2017) 'The long reach of adult bullying: How this kind of harassment can have harmful ripple effects on your body and mind', *U.S. News*, https://health.usnews.com/wellness/mind/articles/2017-12-15/how-adult-bullying-impacts-your-mental-and-physical-heath

Covey, S. R. (2004) *The 7 Habits of Highly Effective People: Powerful lessons in personal change*, Simon & Schuster

Cushard, B. (2016) 'Communicate better: Only 14% of your employees understand your company strategy', https://blog.servicerocket.com/adoption/communicate-better-only-14-of-your-employees-understand-your-company-strategy

Czarnecki, S. (2018) 'Eight in 10 consumers say they're more loyal to purpose-driven brands: Cone', https://www.prweek.com/article/1466208/eight-10-consumers-say-theyre-loyal-purpose-driven-brands-cone

Duggan, M. (2014) 'Online harassment', Pew Research Center

Farbrot, A. (2014) 'Humble leaders get more commitment', BI Norwegian Business School, Sciencenordic.com

Gray, D. (2019) '"A frenzy of self-righteousness": Top Australian businessman laments rise of "intolerant" views', *The Age*

Kiel, F. (2015) 'Return on character', *Harvard Business Review*, April 2015 Issue

Kowalski, R.M., Toth, A. & Morgan, M. (2016) 'Bullying and cyberbullying in adulthood and the workplace', *The Journal of Social Psychology*, vol. 158, no. 1

Llopis, G. (2019) *Leadership in the Age of Personalization: Why standarization fails in the age of 'me'*, GLLG Press

Meier, L.L., Cho, E. & Dumani, S. (2015) 'The effect of positive work reflection during leisure time on affective well-being: Results from three diary studies', *Journal of Organizational Behavior*, John Wiley & Sons, Ltd

Nielsen, M.B., Nielsen, G.H., Notelaers, G. & Einarsen, S., (2015) 'Workplace bullying and suicidal ideation: A 3-wave longitudinal Norwegian study', *American Journal of Public Health*, vol. 105, no. 11

Peterson, J.B. (2018) *12 Rules for Life: An antidote to chaos*, Random House Canada

Porter, J. (2017) 'Why you should make time for self-reflection (even if you hate doing it)', *Harvard Business Review*, https://hbr.org/2017/03/why-you-should-make-time-for-self-reflection-even-if-you-hate-doing-it

'Putting purpose to work: A study of purpose in the workplace' (2016) www.pwc.com

Stefano, G.D., Gino, F., Pisano, G.P. & Staats, B.R. (2016) 'Making experience count: The role of reflection in individual learning', Harvard Business School NOM Unit Working Paper No. 14-093; Harvard Business School Technology & Operations Mgt. Unit Working Paper No. 14-093; HEC Paris Research Paper No. SPE-2016-1181

Sull, D., Turconi, S., Sull, C. & Yoder, J. (2018) 'Turning strategy into results', *MIT Sloan Management Review*, https://sloanreview.mit.edu/article/turning-strategy-into-results/

Witt, D. (2012) 'Only 14% of your employees understand their company's strategy and direction', https://leaderchat.org/2012/05/21/only-14-of-employees-understand-their-companys-strategy-and-direction/

Zak, P.J. (2017) 'The neuroscience of trust', *Harvard Business Review*

Chapter 2

'A world-first look into the psychological safety of Australian employees' (2017) Australian Network On Disability, https://www.and.org.au/articles. php/7/a-world-first-look-into-the-psychological-safety-of-australian-employees

Barsade, S. & O'Neill, O.A. (2014) 'What's love got to do with it? A longitudinal study of the culture of companionate love and employee and client outcomes in a long-term care setting', *Administrative Science Quarterly*, vol. 59, no. 4

Bechervaise, C. (2013) '5 reasons why vision is important in leadership', https://takeitpersonelly.com/2013/10/14/5-reasons-why-vision-is-important-in-leadership/

Biography.com (2018) 'Queen Elizabeth II biography', https://www.biography.com/royalty/queen-elizabeth-ii, A&E Television Networks

Chignell, B. (2018) 'Four ways exercise benefits you at work', https://www.ciphr.com/advice/benefits-of-exercise/

Computer History Museum, 'Timeline of computer history', https://www.computerhistory.org/timeline/networking-the-web/#169ebbe2ad45559efbc6eb35720a1eed

Coulson, J.C., McKenna, J. & Field, M. (2008) 'Exercising at work and self-reported work performance', *International Journal of Workplace Health Management*, vol. 1, no. 3

Draper, L., (2015) 'Duty is the key to the Queen's success', *Newsweek*, https://www.newsweek.com/duty-key-queens-success-328281

Edmondson, A.C. & Lei, Z. (2014) 'Psychological safety: The history, renaissance, and future of an interpersonal construct', *Annual Review of Organizational Psychology and Organizational Behavior*, no. 1

Friedman, R. (2014) 'Regular exercise is part of your job', *Harvard Business Review*

McKeever, V. (2019) 'Billionaire Richard Branson: What being a parent has in common with starting a business', https://www.cnbc.com/2019/11/19/richard-branson-compares-being-a-parent-to-starting-a-business.html

Miller, S.G. (2017) 'Here's why yawns are so contagious', Live Science, https://www.livescience.com/60288-why-are-yawns-so-contagious.html

National Business Group on Health (2019) 'Employees want additional help from employers to improve their financial and mental health', https://www.globenewswire.com/news-release/2019/07/10/1880854/0/en/Employees-Want-Additional-Help-from-Employers-to-Improve-their-Financial-and-Mental-Health.html

Nink, M. (2015) 'Many employees don't know what's expected of them at work', Gallup News, https://news.gallup.com/businessjournal/186164/employees-don-know-expected-work.aspx

Quackenbush, C. (2018) 'Declassified spy papers reveal a 1981 attempt to assassinate Queen Elizabeth II in New Zealand', *Time Magazine*, https://time.com/5180574/queen-elizabeth-new-zealand-assassination-attempt/

Siddiqui, M. (2019) '7 Leadership qualities of Queen Elizabeth II that make her stand out from the crowd', https://www.branex.co.uk/blog/leadership-qualities-of-queen-elizabeth-ii/

Tanner, C., Brügger, A., van Schie, S. & Lebherz, C. (2010) 'Actions speak louder than words: The benefits of ethical behaviors of leaders', *Journal of Psychology*, vol. 218, no. 4

The Royal Household (2020) 'Her Majesty The Queen', https://www.royal.uk/her-majesty-the-queen

Chapter 3

Brown, B. (2018) *Dare to Lead: Brave work. Tough conversations. Whole hearts.* Penguin Random House UK

Covey, S.R. (2004) *The 7 Habits of Highly Effective People: Powerful lessons in personal change*, Simon & Schuster

Devlin, H. (2018) 'Unconscious bias: What is it and can it be eliminated?', *The Guardian*, https://www.theguardian.com/uk-news/2018/dec/02/unconscious-bias-what-is-it-and-can-it-be-eliminated

'Genetics vs. genomics fact sheet' (2018) National Human Genome Research Institute, https://www.genome.gov/about-genomics/fact-sheets/Genetics-vs-Genomics

Robertson, K. (2018) 'Southwest Airlines reveals 5 culture lessons', https://www.humansynergistics.com/blog/culture-university/details/culture-university/2018/05/29/southwest-airlines-reveals-5-culture-lessons

Schwantes, M. (2018) 'How can you tell someone has true leadership skills? This legendary football coach nails it with 1 brilliant sentence', https://www.inc.com/marcel-schwantes/how-can-you-tell-someone-has-true-leadership-skills-this-legendary-football-coach-nails-it-with-1-brilliant-sentence.html

Schwartz, T. (2012) 'New research: How employee engagement hits the bottom line', *Harvard Business Review*

Southwest.com (2020) 'About Southwest', https://www.southwest.com/html/about-southwest/index.html?clk=GFOOTER-ABOUT-ABOUT

Wolpert, S. (2013) 'UCLA neuroscientist's book explains why social connection is as important as food and shelter', https://newsroom.ucla.edu/releases/we-are-hard-wired-to-be-social-248746

Chapter 4

Covey, S.R. (2004) *The 7 Habits of Highly Effective People: Powerful lessons in personal change*, Simon & Schuster

Delizonna, L. (2017) 'High-performing teams need psychological safety. Here's how to create it', *Harvard Business Review*

Frauenheim, E. (2019) 'How Workday focuses on improving its workplace culture every day', *Fortune* magazine, https://fortune.com/2019/01/17/how-workday-focuses-on-improving-its-workplace-culture-every-day/

Kubota, A. (2019) 'Workday ranks #4 on *Fortune*'s list of 100 best companies to work for', https://www.globenewswire.com/news-release/2019/02/14/1725564/0/en/Workday-Ranks-4-on-Fortune-s-List-of-100-Best-Companies-to-Work-For.html

Larson, E. (2017) 'New research: Diversity + inclusion = better decision making at work', https://www.forbes.com/sites/eriklarson/2017/09/21/new-research-diversity-inclusion-better-decision-making-at-work/#4f22cf014cbf

Llopis, G. (2019) *Leadership in the Age of Personalization: Why Standardization fails in the age of 'me'*, GLLG Press

Nink, M. (2015) 'Many employees don't know what's expected of them at work', Gallup News, https://news.gallup.com/businessjournal/186164/employees-don-know-expected-work.aspx

Ridgway, A. (2018) 'People management: How to create a psychologically safe environment at work', https://www.hrzone.com/lead/culture/people-management-how-to-create-a-psychologically-safe-environment-at-work

Solomon, L. (2015) 'New Interact report: Many leaders shrink from straight talk with employees', http://interactauthentically.com/new-interact-report-many-leaders-shrink-from-straight-talk-with-employees/

Sutton, R. & Wigert, B. (2019) 'More harm than good: The truth about performance reviews', Gallup, https://www.gallup.com/workplace/249332/harm-good-truth-performance-reviews.aspx

Titus, A., 'Why workplace friendships are essential to employee engagement', https://chronus.com/blog/why-workplace-friendships-essential-employee-engagement

Workday.com, https://www.workday.com/en-au/company/about-workday.html

Workday Stock Profile, https://www.macroaxis.com/invest/market/WDAY--Workday-Inc

Zak, P.J. (2017) 'The neuroscience of trust', *Harvard Business Review*

Chapter 5

Australian Institute of Health and Welfare (2018) 'Australia's health 2018: In brief'. Cat. no. AUS 222

Boeldt, M. (2017) 'How engaged workers are safe employees', https://www.ehstoday.com/safety/article/21919203/how-engaged-workers-are-safe-employees

Chignell, B. (2018) 'Four ways exercise benefits you at work', https://www.ciphr.com/advice/benefits-of-exercise/

Coulson, J.C., McKenna, J. & Field, M. (2008) 'Exercising at work and self-reported work performance', *International Journal of Workplace Health Management*, vol. 1, no. 3, https://www.researchgate.net/publication/235275530_Exercising_at_work_and_self-reported_work_performance

Frank Dando Sports Academy, https://www.fdsa.vic.edu.au/our-school

Friedman, R. (2014) 'Regular exercise is part of your job', *Harvard Business Review*

Goetzel, R.Z., Ozminkowski, R.J., Bruno, J.A., Rutter, K.R., Isaac, F. & Wang, S. (2002) 'The long-term impact of Johnson & Johnson's Health & Wellness Program on employee health risks', *Journal of Occupational and Environmental Medicine*, vol. 44, no. 5

Hilton, J. (2018) 'We set a goal to have the world's healthiest workforce by 2020', https://www.hcamag.com/au/news/general/we-set-a-goal-to-have-the-worlds-healthiest-workforce-by-2020/152991

Johnson & Johnson, 'Our heritage', https://www.jnj.com/our-heritage

McGibbon, A. & Gillespie, K. (2018) 'Not another diet fad – how to eat your way to better mental health', https://www.myglws.com/files/2019/01/Not-another-diet-fad.pdf

Oppezzo, M. & Schwartz, D.L. (2014) 'Give your ideas some legs: The positive effect of walking on creating thinking', *Journal of Experimental Psychology: Learning, Memory, and Cognition*, vol. 40, no. 4

Pich, D. & Messenger, A. (2019) *Leading Well: 7 attributes of very successful leaders*, Institute of Managers & Leaders, Major Street Publishing Pty Ltd

'Regular exercise could boost creativity' (2013), *HuffPost*, https://www.huffpost.com/entry/exercise-creativity-physical-activity_n_4394310

Seppälä, E. & Cameron, K. (2015) 'Proof that positive work cultures are more productive', *Harvard Business Review*

Stahl, A. (2017) 'The links between diet and productivity', https://www.forbes.com/sites/ashleystahl/2017/09/08/the-links-between-diet-and-productivity/#89fa7ff667ab

Wasley, A. (2016) 'Should we all have a standing desk?' https://www.bodyandsoul.com.au/health/health-news/should-we-all-have-a-standing-desk/news-story/87d6fbde640c8963089944f3e2fe3ac9?utm_source=SEM&utm_

medium=cpc&gclid=EAIaIQobChMIh-nOtsGb5wIVQo6
PCh2BpQa3EAMYAiAAEgI5-fD_BwE

Chapter 6

Born, W. (2019) *The Languages of Leadership: How to use your words, actions and behaviours to influence your team, peers and boss*, Major Street Publishing Pty Ltd

Cothran, J. (2017) 'Don't be afraid to change your company values', https://www.small-improvements.com/blog/changing-company-values/

Di Stefano, G., Gino, F., Pisano, G.P. & Staats, B.R. (2016) 'Making experience count: The role of reflection in individual learning', Harvard Business School NOM Unit Working Paper No. 14-093

Forrester, G. (2019) 'Survey says the most trusted leader in Australia is… Jacinda Ardern?' https://www.stuff.co.nz/national/politics/112612868/survey-says-the-most-trusted-leader-in-australia-is-jacinda-ardern

Glaser, J.E. (2014) *Conversational Intelligence: How great leaders build trust and get extraordinary results*, Bibliomotion, Inc. USA

Heifetz, R.A. & Linsky, M. (2002) *Leadership on the Line: Staying alive through the dangers of leading*, Harvard Business Review Press, USA

Lester, A. (2019) 'The roots of Jacinda Ardern's extraordinary leadership after Christchurch', *The New Yorker*, https://www.newyorker.com/culture/culture-desk/what-jacinda-arderns-leadership-means-to-new-zealand-and-to-the-world

Miller, N. (2018) 'We updated our core values for the first time in 5 years, here's how we did it', https://open.buffer.com/values/

Rowland, D. (2016) 'Why leadership development isn't developing leaders', *Harvard Business Review*

Shukla, V. (2019) 'Top 10 greatest leaders of 2019: Setting the benchmark for others', https://www.valuewalk.com/2019/08/top-10-greatest-leaders-of-2019-setting-the-benchmark-for-others/

Thean, P. (2016) '3 reasons to update your core values', https://chiefexecutive.net/3-reasons-change-core-values/

Weller, C. (2019) 'Why it's so hard to speak up at work – and what to do about it', https://neuroleadership.com/your-brain-at-work/speaking-up-at-work/

Chapter 7

Au-Yeung, A. (2018) 'Patagonia's billionaire founder to give away the millions his company saved from Trump's tax cuts to save the planet', https://www.forbes.com/sites/angelauyeung/2018/11/29/patagonias-billionaire-founder-to-give-away-the-millions-his-company-saved-thanks-to-tax-cuts/#82f77431d6f3

Danao, M. (2018) 'How Patagonia became a $1B retail powerhouse… with a heart', https://www.referralcandy.com/blog/patagonia-marketing-strategy/

Denny, J. (2017) 'Why your employees should know the business mission', https://www.growthengineering.co.uk/benefits-communicating-business-mission/

Dolan, G. (2019) *Real Communication: How to be you and lead true*, John Wiley & Sons Australia, Ltd

Dvorak, N. (2017) 'Three ways mission-driven workplaces perform better', Gallup https://www.gallup.com/workplace/236279/three-ways-mission-driven-workplaces-perform-better.aspx

Health, A. (2019) 'Spotlight on Patagonia: Core values key to employee engagement', https://wethrive.net/blog/spotlight-patagonia-core-values-key-employee-engagement/

Kaplan, R.S. & Norton, D.P. (2005) 'The office of strategy management', *Harvard Business Review*

Kause, P. (2016) 'So (you and) your people don't understand your strategy?', https://www.fibresonline.com/so-you-and-your-people-dont-understand-your-strategy/

Lencioni, P. (2012) *The Advantage: Why organizational health trumps everything else in business*, Jossey-Bass, USA

MacKinnon, J.B. (2015) 'Patagonia's anti-growth strategy', *The New Yorker*, https://www.newyorker.com/business/currency/patagonias-anti-growth-strategy?verso=true

Ratanjee, V. (2018) 'How to get people behind a new company vision', Gallup, https://www.gallup.com/workplace/240644/people-behind-new-company-vision.aspx

Russell, E. & Underwood, C. (2016) 'Exploring the role of purpose in leadership', https://www.hrmagazine.co.uk/article-details/exploring-the-role-of-purpose-in-leadership

Tipler, C.J. (2010) *Corpus RIOS: The how and what of business strategy*, Bambra Press, Australia

Chapter 8

Australian Bureau of Statistics, 'Household and family projections, Australia, 2016 to 2041', https://www.abs.gov.au/ausstats/abs@.nsf/mf/3236.0

Fortune Editors (2014) 'The world's 50 greatest leaders (2014)', https://fortune.com/2014/03/20/worlds-50-greatest-leaders/

Garner, J. (2017) *It's Who You Know: How a network of 12 key people can fast-track your success*, John Wiley & Sons Australia, Ltd

Kiel, F. (2015) *Return on Character: The real reason leaders and their companies win*, Harvard Business Review Press

Patterson, K., Grenny, J., McMillan, R. & Switzler, A. (2012) *Crucial Conversations: Tools for talking when stakes are high*, McGraw-Hill

'The benefits of a mentoring relationship', (accessed 2020) Professional Development, University of Southampton, https://www.southampton.ac.uk/professional-development/mentoring/benefits-of-a-mentoring-relationship.page

INDEX

ALSO BY WENDY BORN

Many of us have issues trying to lead disparate teams with multiple personalities, colleagues with conflicting agendas and bosses with minds of their own. The questions we often ask ourselves are: How do I manage my team leaders?; How do I manage my peers? How do I manage my own leader to stop making big promises to my team that I know they won't deliver on?

The
LANGUAGES
of **LEADERSHIP**

*How to use your
words, actions
and behaviours to
influence your team,
peers and boss*

WENDY BORN

The answer is to learn to master the languages of leadership. In this fascinating book, Wendy Born will show you how and teach you to make small changes that will have a big impact.

The Languages of Leadership is available from all good bookstores and from the publisher **majorstreet.com.au**

Notes

Notes

Notes

Notes

Notes

www.ingramcontent.com/pod-product-compliance
Lightning Source LLC
Chambersburg PA
CBHW060551210326
41519CB00014B/3439